D0112604

THE SUSTAINABLE TRAVEL HANDBOOK

Practical advice and inspiration for the conscientious traveller

© MATT MUNRO / LONELY PLANET

CONTENTS

PLANNING YOUR TRIP

TAKING THE LEAP

ON THE ROAD

INSPIRATION

AFTER YOUR TRIP

© PHILIP LEE HARVEY / LONELY PLANET

TAKING
THE LEAP

The time to travel sustainably is now

No longer an activity reserved for a privileged few, travel has become more accessible than ever. And while this access comes with many benefits, the coronavirus crisis that brought international travel to a halt in 2020 provided an extraordinary insight into the toll our travel habits have taken on the planet.

Growing concern about the negative effects of tourism has given rise to the concept of sustainable travel. Defined by the United Nations World Tourism Organization (UNWTO) as 'tourism that takes full account of its current and future economic, social and environmental impacts, addressing the needs of visitors, the industry, the environment and host communities', sustainable tourism delivers meaningful visitor experiences while at the same time benefiting local people and the environment, both today and in the future. It works hand in hand with responsible travel in that sustainability is the shared goal, which travellers can help to achieve by making more responsible travel decisions on the road.

The global tourism industry has made great strides towards sustainability in recent years, with thousands of tourism businesses worldwide continuing to evolve in line with changing consumer attitudes. On top of having a memorable trip, travellers increasingly want to do right by the places they visit.

What it actually means to travel sustainably, however, can be confusing. Given that the simple act of travelling creates carbon emissions, perhaps the most important lesson is that sustainable travel is all about effort, not perfection. This point is reflected in our book, which is designed to give you the tools you need to endeavour to travel more sustainably.

The tips, ideas and information featured in The Sustainable Travel Handbook prove that sustainable tourism is possible anywhere and can take many forms, from choosing destinations that value sustainable practices to supporting local businesses. Perhaps most importantly, this book reveals that travelling sustainably isn't all that difficult.

Don't know where to start? We begin by exploring some of the major questions about sustainable and responsible travel and move on to provide practical data and advice for planning and booking more sustainable trips. You'll also find out how to minimise your impact on the road and how to encourage more travellers to join the movement.

Ready to travel more sustainably? Check out our sustainable holiday suggestions to inspire your next low-impact adventure, from the world's most thrilling electric road trips to detailed destination guides with insider tips on how to tap into different regions' sustainable tourism potential. Scattered throughout the book are eco-hacks designed to make sustainable travel even easier, as well as advice from sustainable tourism experts on topics ranging from how to take more responsible travel photos to navigating some of the ethical dilemmas you may encounter en route.

We hope that this book will prompt you to reassess your travel habits and inspire you to choose travel experiences that deliver long-lasting memories, while also helping to safeguard local culture and the environment in the wonderful places you visit.

Learning the lingo

So many catchphrases have entered the eco-lexicon that it can be confusing figuring out what each means and which one to use. This quick reference guide will help you out.

© RANCHO MASTATAL

SUSTAINABLE TRAVEL

The United Nations World Tourism Organization (UNWTO) defines sustainable tourism as, 'tourism that takes full account of its current and future economic, social and environmental impacts, addressing the needs of visitors, the industry, the environment and host communities.' In a nutshell, it's tourism that delivers a memorable guest experience while making a sustainable positive impact on the triple bottom line: the environment, the local people and the local economy.

RESPONSIBLE TRAVEL

Defined in 2002 at the Cape Town Conference on Responsible Tourism in Destinations, responsible travel is about, 'making better places for people to live in and better places for people to visit'. At their most basic, sustainable and responsible travel share the same objectives. But they're slightly different in that responsible travel puts the onus on the individual traveller to be aware of their impact – in doing so, they'll be engaging with the wider principles of sustainable travel. As renowned US sustainable tourism expert Dr Harold Goodwin explains: 'sustainability is the goal, a goal which can only be achieved by people taking responsibility together to achieve it'.

ECOTOURISM

In 1990, The International Ecotourism Society (TIES) defined ecotourism as 'responsible travel to natural areas that conserves the environment and improves the well-being of local people'. The term has since been adapted to denote tourism to natural areas, including tourism which may not have a positive impact. It was perhaps for this reason that in 2015 TIES updated its definition to, 'responsible travel to natural areas that conserves the environment, sustains the well-being of the local people, and involves interpretation and education.' So 'authentic' ecotourism is essentially a subset of sustainable travel, focusing on the natural world.

ECO-HOTEL

Just like ecotourism, the term 'eco-hotel' has been adapted to describe lodgings located in natural areas that may not necessarily be sustainable. A true eco-hotel (or green hotel) is an environmentally sustainable accommodation designed to minimise its impact on the natural environment.

GREEN TRAVEL

Green travel is a broad term that typically refers to environmentally conscious travel but may also refer to other aspects of sustainable travel. This term is often used a substitute for sustainable or responsible travel.

© SECRET BAY'S ZABUCO VILLA

DECODING SUSTAINABLE TOURISM CERTIFICATION

Designed to assure consumers that tourism businesses have met a set of minimum standards, sustainability certification is the key indicator of a truly sustainable tourism product.

Sustainable tourism certification is still a relatively new concept. Formed in 2007, the not-for-profit organisation now known as the Global Sustainable Tourism Council (GSTC) released criteria for certifying destinations in 2013 – these range from monitoring visitor numbers to adopting strategies for addressing climate change and protecting local heritage sites – followed by the release of its industry (hotel and tour operator) criteria in 2016. This prompted other organisations to develop their own sustainable tourism certification criteria. Many of these have since sought accreditation from the GSTC to boost their credibility as certifiers (searchable via the GSTC website; www.gstcouncil.org). Some of the most common certifiers you may encounter include EarthCheck, Green Globe and Green Key, but there are many more.

Keep in mind that meeting the requirements of top certification programmes can be out of financial reach for some small tourism businesses, particularly in developing regions.

Randy Durband, CEO of the GSTC, recommends consumers do not overlook 'operators that do most things "right" in terms of sustainability, and are transparent about their strengths and their weaknesses'.

WHAT ABOUT SUSTAINABLE CERTIFICATION FOR HOTELS?

There are now hundreds of sustainability certifications for the built environment which recognise the practice of designing, constructing and operating buildings to maximise occupant health, use fewer resources, reduce waste and negative environmental impacts, and decrease life-cycle costs. The most widely used is Leadership in Energy and Environmental Design (LEED), developed by the US Green Building Council. Across the pond, the British BREEAM (Building Research Establishment Environmental Assessment Method) system tends to be more common. Many new hotel developments around the world have also embraced the Cradle to Cradle model that seeks to ensure development is not only sustainable but essentially waste-free.

© DEREK GALON / JWA ROOM

CONSCIOUS TRAVEL

There's no one definition of conscious travel to rule them all, but the basic concept is to travel in a way that is environmentally sustainable, socially just and spiritually fulfilling. In effect, it's a form of sustainable tourism that focuses more on the role of the traveller to make a positive impact.

ETHICAL OR MINDFUL TRAVEL

Similar to conscious travel, ethical or mindful travel is about being mindful of our travel choices, based on our awareness of moral values and the impacts of the travel decisions we make. The ethical part pertains to the experience, rather than to the traveller. For example, you might not have a moral issue with riding elephants, but it would be unethical to ride an elephant in Thailand due to the animal-welfare issues involved with the activity.

SLOW TRAVEL

An evolution of the slow food movement, which was born out of a protest against the opening of a McDonald's restaurant in Rome in 1986, slow travel is all about appreciating the moment. The idea is that by slowing down and connecting to nature and people, travellers experience the destination more deeply and authentically. This type of travel typically also benefits local people and the environment, but not always.

COMMUNITY-BASED TOURISM

Community-based tourism (CBT) is tourism owned and/or managed by communities and intended to deliver wider community benefit. It sees local residents hosting visitors, offering them a deeper experiential and participatory insight into local culture and the environment than they would otherwise receive. As a key stakeholder, the community has more control over the experience, and therefore accrues more benefits.

VOLUNTOURISM

The blending of 'volunteering' and 'tourism', voluntourism means taking a working holiday for social and environmental causes, while experiencing integration with culture, community and conservation. Voluntourists are integral to many organisations doing wonderful things, but not all volunteering organisations were created equal. Take a look at the checklist on p11 before signing up to any project.

© SECRET BAY

How to see through greenwashing

The term 'greenwashing' was coined in the 1980s to describe misleading corporate environmental claims. Three decades later, the practice has grown more sophisticated – particularly in the travel industry.

Have you ever felt tricked into booking a tourism product that wasn't as ecofriendly as it seemed? Perhaps your hotel claimed to be committed to minimising its water usage yet washed your linen daily. Or a tour operator decorated its web pages with leaves and trees to suggest its tours had a smaller footprint than they really did.

Welcome to the ugly side of sustainable tourism. As the movement gains momentum, many businesses have resorted to using sneaky marketing tactics to promote tourism products or policies as sustainable (or simply ecofriendly) when in fact they are not.

Pretending to adhere to the concept of sustainable tourism and not actually follow through is damaging on various levels, says Milena Nikolova, traveller behaviour expert and Director of Knowledge and AdventureEDU at the Adventure Travel Trade Association.

'It is harmful for travellers who trust that the money they spend with a tourism business has a positive impact on the environment, and it is harmful for communities because they see their nature suffer from an irresponsibly managed footprint,' Nikolova says.

SPOT THE WARNING SIGNS

Avoid being duped by keeping your eye out for these common greenwashing tactics.

Vague claims:

Just because a tour company promotes an 'eco-tour' or an accommodation calls itself an 'eco-hotel', it doesn't necessarily mean they operate sustainably. If the company's sustainability claims are poorly defined or too broad, ask for clarification. Companies that care will be more than happy to talk you through their policies.

Missing proof:

Perhaps the company claims it has been certified by a sustainable travel organisation, has won awards for its green policies, or has been recommended by Lonely Planet. Be cautious of any business that can't back up these claims with recent proof.

Unsustainable socials:

Check out the businesses' website and social media feeds. If it takes sustainability seriously, you won't see pictures of tourists feeding or riding wild animals, hotels full of single-use plastics, buffets overflowing with food and so on.

Lack of locals:

Sustainable tourism businesses should help to make a positive difference in the local community. This can be done in many ways, but typically involves employing local people (fairly), using local products and supporting community-based initiatives.

© BRAVO RESORT

PLANNING YOUR TRIP

The great air travel debate

With a single long-haul flight generating more carbon emissions than the average person in many countries produces in a whole year, flying is the biggest emission contributor for most individuals. But what's a globetrotter to do? Those concerned by the effects of air travel can start by getting wise to the issue and the options available.

Flying currently accounts for about 2% of global emissions, and with passenger numbers projected to double to 8.2 billion in 2037, climate experts believe we must halve our global emissions by 2030 and reach net zero by 2050 to have any chance of limiting global warming to the 1.5°C target outlined in the 2015 Paris Agreement. While ecofriendly innovations such as biofuels offer hope, they are outpaced by the growth of the aviation sector. In other words, now is the time to start scrutinising your approach to air travel.

Far from meaning an end to travel, a commitment to flying less can open up new horizons. Train journeys, electric vehicles, low-impact cruises, cycle tours, buses and even hiking all offer incredible ways to get from A to B at a lower emission cost, while at the same time creating opportunities to experience your destination more deeply.

© KOOLYPHOTO / SHUTTERSTOCK

DO WE REALLY NEED TO GIVE UP FLYING?

Before the coronavirus pandemic grounded flights worldwide, support for the no-fly movement, a global community of people giving up air travel due to the carbon cost, was growing. The issue has been significant among environmental scientists for years, but the movement rose to prominence in 2017 when Swedish singer Staffan Lindberg coined the term flygskam, or flight shame, and pledged to give up flying. Fellow Swede and environmental activist Greta Thunberg then put that principle into action in 2019 when she crossed the Atlantic by yacht to attend the United Nations climate summit in New York, before sailing on to the COP25 climate meeting in Madrid.

While signing up to the no-fly movement might be the single most effective thing you can do to lower your personal emissions, critics argue that flying provides an opportunity for regular people to experience the world, that flygskam is a middle-class movement impractical for those unable to commit time and money to alternatives such as train travel, and that in vast, remote countries like Australia, giving up flying is simply not feasible. The takeaway? If you must fly, try to make it count.

FLYING SMART

Dreaming of your next trip but worried about the impact of flying? Making small changes and planet-conscious choices can reduce your carbon footprint.

Travel light

Extra weight on planes burns fuel faster. According to the UN's Environment Programme, reducing the weight of your luggage by 15kg decreases your emissions by around 50 to 100kg on a 4½-hour flight. Tempted to upgrade to business class? Be aware that economy has the least environmental cost as it carries more people for the same amount of fuel.

Go direct and stay longer

With 25% of aeroplane emissions occurring during take-off and landing, flying point-to-point without stopovers is the best way

© PHILIP LEE HARVEY / LONELY PLANET

© ATIT PHETMUANGTONG/EYEEM / GETTY IMAGES

to reduce your carbon emissions. Staying longer and travelling overland once you've arrived is also friendlier on the planet than taking short internal flights.

Choose your plane wisely

Non-profit Atmosfair (www. atmosfair.de/en) has an Airline Index that ranks carriers by their fuel efficiency. Even better, look at your itinerary to evaluate the actual plane you'll be flying in (newer models are usually more

fuel-efficient). Flight comparison site Skyscanner (www.skyscanner. com) highlights flights with lower emissions.

Offset your carbon emissions

While flying less, or not at all, is a far more impactful option, offsetting your carbon emissions is arguably the best thing you can do to negate the effects of flying. For the ultimate lowdown on carbon offsetting, flip to p20.

THE ELECTRIC REVOLUTION

WILL FREQUENT FLYER TAXES TAKE OFF?

In 2019, France became the first country to propose an 'eco-tax' of at least €1.50 on all flights departing its airports, with revenue earmarked to improve public transport networks. Meanwhile, a frequent flyer levy has been floated in the UK, with the idea that those who fly the most, pay the most. With activists claiming the French tax is too low to change consumer behaviour, time will tell how eco-taxes evolve in the aviation industry.

While it could be decades before electric or even hybrid-electric long-haul flights become a reality, electric aircraft technology is rapidly developing around the world.

© BLOOMBERG / GETTY IMAGES

In the US, Boeing-backed Zunum Aero is working on a 12-seat hybrid-electric commuter aircraft to take wing in the early 2020s, with a 50-seater to follow at the end of the decade. Airbus is developing a 19-seat hybrid aircraft for the early 2020s, and also has plans for a 100-seat hybrid-electric electro-liner based on NASA technology.

In a world-first, an all-electric seaplane took its inaugural flight in Vancouver in December 2019. Pending regulatory approvals, Canadian seaplane operator Harbour Air hopes to electrify its entire fleet by 2022. Meanwhile, Israeli start-up Eviation aims to have its first nine-seater commuter plane in commercial service on regional routes in 2021. In partnership with UK budget airline Easyjet, LA start-up Wright Electric also aspires to have a 180-seat electric airliner flying routes of up to 480km (300 miles) by 2027.

As for getting to and from the airport, Uber Air plans to begin commercial operations of its electric flying taxi service in 2023, following tests in Melbourne, Dallas and Los Angeles. Scheduled to launch its own commercial flights in 2025, German aviation start-up Lilium completed the first phase of testing on its five-seater electrically powered flying car, the Lilium Jet, in late 2019.

The lowdown on carbon offsetting

About a third of airlines offer customers the option of offsetting their share of the carbon emissions generated by their chosen flight, but the International Air Transport Association (IATA) claims only around 1% of passengers sign up. For many, the biggest barrier is a lack of information about how offsetting works. So we've broken it down.

How are carbon offsets calculated?

Calculations vary between airlines. Usually they take the total carbon emissions produced by your flight, based on past fuel usage, and divide it by the number of seats on the plane.

This is then multiplied by the cost of offsetting one tonne of carbon, according to their carbon offset scheme. So shorter trips work out cheaper, even though short-haul flights burn more fuel per kilometre over the course of a flight (because take-offs off and landings are more fuel-intensive than cruising).

BOOK GREENER FLIGHTS

Glooby: The website touts itself as the first platform that facilitates booking low-carbon flights and ecofriendly hotels. www.glooby.com
Flygrn: Compare and book flights, then allow Flygrn to carbon offset your flights with tree or solar projects for free. www.flygrn.com
Skyscanner: The flight comparison website displays 'greener choice' indicators for flight itineraries that emit substantially less carbon than other options listed. www.skyscanner.com

Where does the money go?

Airlines direct it to carbon offset projects, ideally without charging a fee for doing so. Most projects fall into two categories: forestry initiatives like replanting trees or preventing them being cut down, and energy efficiency initiatives such as renewable energy projects. Benefiting communities and the environment, the latter tends to have greater impact.

How can you be sure the offset scheme works?

As a 2017 EU study found that 85% of offset projects overestimated their impact or failed to reduce carbon emissions at all, it pays to research what you're signing up to, says Dr Roger Tyers, a sociology Research Fellow in at the UK's University of Southampton whose PHD thesis explored carbon offsetting.

'Everyone loves the idea of planting trees, but trees don't grow fast enough to absorb the volume of carbon currently being pumped into the atmosphere', Tyers says, adding that less glamorous carbon reduction schemes can be more effective: 'Projects that capture methane gas from landfill have proven to be very successful'.

If your airline isn't transparent about the project it works with, Tyers suggests offsetting through an organisation such as Atmosfair (www.atmosfair.de), which supports renewable energy projects. 'It's a bit

TRAVEL OPERATORS VS CARBON

A growing number of travel operators are offering to offset carbon emissions on behalf of holidaymakers, while others are taking it to the next level.

Trekking and adventure company World Expeditions (www.worldexpeditions.com) is one of the latest major international operators to make its trips carbon-neutral through offsetting, while Intrepid Travel (www.intrepidtravel.com), which has been carbon-neutral since 2010, became a climate-positive company in 2020, meaning it goes beyond achieving neutral status to take action to remove additional CO_2 from the atmosphere. On top of offsetting, it helps to fund carbon reduction projects including a seaweed-based carbon drawdown scheme in Tasmania, Australia.

But not all mindful travel companies agree with carbon offsetting. Tour aggregator Responsible Travel (www.responsibletravel. com) introduced an offsetting scheme in 2002 before dropping it in 2009, with founder Justin Francis claiming offsetting would 'delay the need for urgent innovation and investment by allowing the continued use of emissions-intensive fuels'. Taking a different approach, in 2020 UK-based operator Much Better Adventures (www. muchbetteradventures.com) founded Tourism Declares a Climate Emergency (www.tourismdeclares.com), a collective of 89 travel companies that have declared an emergency and are working together to find solutions to the climate crisis.

more expensive, but that's because their calculations are generally more honest', says Tyers.

Before deciding on any offsetting programme, look for certification by the likes of Gold Standard (www. goldstandard.org) and the baseline standards of the organisation's projects.

So is it worth buying carbon offsets?

Environmentalists claim offsetting serves to offset travellers' guilt, rather than encourage a change in flying habits. However, Tyers asserts that it's better than doing nothing: 'While offsetting should be treated with caution, we need to act on climate change however we can'. Tyers believes that the aviation industry has the biggest role to play: '[It] doesn't pay tax on jet fuel, so there is no financial incentive for it to invest heavily in biofuels and other more ecofriendly technology. If you look at the sales forecasts on the Boeing website, they're going to be selling emissions-intensive jets for decades.'

So is there a more effective alternative to offsetting? Tyers believes that redirecting carbon offset costs to a humanitarian organisation might have a greater impact than donating to an airline offsetting schemes.

'Carbon offsetting should be seen as a charitable donation, and if we want to give to a charity, perhaps we should consider donating to organisations like the International Red Cross or Doctors Without Borders that work in the developing world where people are currently reliant on a fossil fuel lifestyle', Tyers says.

Choosing your destination

Travel has long been viewed as a benign activity, but with nearly 1.5 billion people packing their bags each year, the impact on many destinations is now far from gentle. One way to reduce this is to opt for more sustainable destinations, but you can travel sustainably in a place that perhaps isn't so sustainable itself. Considering when and how you travel is key.

Should we travel to endangered destinations?

From the gondola gridlocks of Venice to the melting ice caps of Mt Kilimanjaro, some of the world's most beautiful and culturally unique places are under threat due to climate change, globalisation and other consequences of human behaviour. But by rushing to see them before they're gone, could you be contributing to their ultimate demise?

On the one hand, last-chance tourism raises public awareness of the climate crisis and overtourism. Advocates of travelling to endangered destinations also argue that the simple act of experiencing inspires people to protect. Yet critics claim the effect of tourism on particularly fragile destinations (such as Peru's Machu Picchu, where ancient stone paths and steps are being eroded by the sheer number of visitors walking on them, despite a new ticketing system introduced to mitigate the damage) outweighs the awareness raised, and that the difference between understanding the issues and taking action to help remedy them remains wide.

If you do go, taking every action to minimise your own impact is crucial. You may also wish to donate to foundations dedicated to maintaining and restoring the sites you visit, on top of paying the conservation fees built into the ticket price.

ECO-HACK

Off-peak travel tends to be cheaper and can help minimise your impact on the destination. With a calendar colour-coded by price bracket/demand and alerts for cheap flights just outside of your preferred travel dates, the Hopper app makes booking off-peak travel a cinch. www. hopper.com

© PATRICK ORTON / GETTY IMAGES

© ALEKSANDRA KOSSOWSKA / ALAMY STOCK PHOTO

WHAT MAKES A DESTINATION SUSTAINABLE?

In 2019 the Pacific island nation of Palau was ranked the world's most sustainable tourism destination at international travel trade show ITB Berlin, in recognition of its forward-thinking earth-friendly initiatives. The South American nation of Guyana was also recognised for its unique approach to ecotourism, while the Maltese island of Gozo received a nod for its efforts to safeguard its culture. But can a destination ever be truly sustainable?

Requiring continuing commitment and ongoing collaboration among a wide range of stakeholders, achieving sustainable destination status is surely something of a never-ending journey? Yet destinations striving towards sustainability are certainly worthy of your support. To date just 13 destinations have been deemed sustainable by a certifying body accredited by the Global Sustainable Tourism Council. From whale-watching tours in Kaikoura in New Zealand to world-class skiing in Vail, Colorado, to exploring the volcanic landscape of Iceland's Snæfellsnes Peninsula, all offer compelling reasons to visit beyond their sustainable status. With coronavirus travel restrictions creating an unexpected opportunity for destinations around the world to rethink their tourism management strategies, with any luck we may see many more destinations added to this list in future.

© BLAKE81 / GETTY IMAGES

Six things every sustainable traveller should know before you go

As thrilling as the idea of dropping everything and jumping on a plane might be, neglecting to research your destination before you arrive increases the risk of causing damage. Arm yourself with the answers to the following questions before you go to ensure you have the know-how to navigate your destination more responsibly.

★ What local laws, social issues and cultural etiquette should I be aware of?
★ How do I say hello, please and thank you in the local dialect?
★ Which businesses in my destination are local-owned and sustainable?
★ Does the destination have unsustainable tourism experiences I should avoid?
★ Are there environmental issues such as water shortages I should be aware of?
★ Is it possible to drink the tap water to avoid buying bottled?

Eight ways to counter overtourism

Overtourism is a term used to describe destinations that have been environmentally or culturally degraded by excess tourism. As more destinations struggle to manage the volume of tourists they receive, every traveller has a responsibility to tread extra carefully. Here are some tips on how to reduce the strain on busy places, which will also stand you in good stead wherever you travel.

★ Visit during off-peak periods
★ Consider regional alternatives
★ Use local-owned businesses
★ Avoid aggravating the region's environmental challenges

★ Respect local people, culture and laws
★ Use a responsible small-group tour operator
★ Try to get off the beaten track, ideally with the help of a guide
★ Travel for yourself, not to get validation from others

REBIRTH OF THE STAYCATION

It didn't enter common usage until the late 2000s, but the 'staycation' concept dates back to 1944, when a US newspaper urged readers to conserve gasoline for the war effort by holidaying closer to home. Today, staycations are sensibly being promoted as a great way to avoid using climate-altering fossil fuels full stop.

THE RIGHT OPERATOR

By booking with an operator committed to sustainability, you can kick back and enjoy the sustainable journey. Flip to p26 for the lowdown on how to choose a responsible operator.

How to choose a responsible tour operator

There's no denying that planning a sustainable trip can take a bit of legwork, particularly for travel to remote destinations and developing countries. So why not recruit a responsible operator to do it for you?

If you prefer to travel independently, chances are you will still use operators for short excursions along the way. Here's some key information to help ensure operators you travel with will help to minimise your impact on your destination.

What does it mean to take a responsible tour?

'By travelling with a tour operator that's genuinely committed to operating responsibly, the fundamentals of supporting local communities and limiting your environmental footprint will have already been built in to your trip', says James Thornton, CEO of small-group tour company Intrepid Travel (www.intrepidtravel.com), known for its pioneering responsible tourism strategies such as being the first major international travel company to remove elephant rides from its tours.

'When you take a responsible tour you are ensuring that the money you spend benefits the local community', echoes Justin Francis, CEO of UK-based Responsible Travel (www.responsibletravel.com), which sells tours from more than 400 specialist operators around the world.

Is it possible to responsibly tour destinations with poor ethical records?

'Travelling responsibly is less about the destination but more about what you do when you get there', says Francis. 'It's possible to travel in an extremely damaging way in countries with even the greatest commitments to human rights and the environment.'

Kelly Galaski, Director of Global Programs for the Planeterra Foundation, the not-for-profit partner of international small-group tour company G Adventures (www.gadventures.com), agrees. 'By experiencing different places and cultures in the most responsible way possible, travellers can become advocates for bettering our world when they return to their home countries', she says. 'Responsible travel operators are crucial in connecting travellers to business owners that are creating opportunities for many at the grassroots level.'

Identifying responsible travel operators

In recent years, many operators have overhauled their offerings to make sure they are more responsible and sustainable. Checking the operator's website for a responsible or sustainable tourism policy is the easiest way to assess its credentials.

These policies typically reflect the World Tourism Organization's definition of sustainable tourism, and may also incorporate additional measures based on the company's own research, or that of non-governmental organisations and academic bodies. Since removing elephant rides from its tours, for example, Intrepid Travel (www.intrepidtravel.com) has also taken measures to secure the safety of vulnerable children in communities that it visits.

'We want to create the best possible experiences for our travellers while ensuring the places we visit are impacted positively,' comments James Thornton. 'That's why instead of including visits to schools or orphanages which pose risks to children, we'll eat and shop at social enterprise restaurants and stores whose earnings fund programs to help keep families together.'

Key ingredients of a responsible tour

★ Low-impact wildlife experiences such as viewing animals in the wild, and visits to legitimate wildlife sanctuaries.
★ Cultural visits that benefit local communities first, and visitors second.
★ Community tourism that keeps children safe and families together (read: no orphanage visits or experiences that support child labour).
★ Accommodation in homestays and boutique properties.
★ Dining experiences based around seasonal local produce, local cultural traditions and local-owned establishments.
★ Local guides who are appropriately trained, outfitted and paid for the services they provide.
★ Waste-minimising initiatives such as offering clients reusable alternatives to common single-use plastics like carrier bags and water bottles.

TOP RESPONSIBLE TOUR BOOKING WEBSITES

★ **Responsible Travel:** Choose from thousands of tours around the world – from family wildlife safaris to off-the-beaten-track cultural journeys – assessed against the aggregator's strict responsible tourism policy. www.responsibletravel.com

★ **Urban Adventures:** Plan your perfect day hosted by a local guide in more than 150 cities on Intrepid Travel's day trip booking platform, which maintains equally high responsible tourism standards. Urban Adventures also works hand in hand with Lonely Planet on a range of single and multi-day small-group tours, Lonely Planet Experiences, all of which are carbon-neutral. www.urbanadventures.com; www.lonelyplanet.com/experiences

★ **Airbnb Experiences:** Some major tour aggregators have failed to deliver on promises to cut cruel wildlife tourism experiences. In collaboration with World Animal Protection, Airbnb committed to selling responsible tours from the outset when it launched animal experiences in 2019. www.airbnb.com/experiences

How to book a genuinely sustainable hotel

With the hotel industry accounting for around 1% of global emissions, it's more important than ever to sleep green.

Gone are the days when a vague commitment to conserving water and electricity (typically in the form of a little card in your hotel bathroom) was the marker of an ecofriendly hotel. Today, a growing number of tourism accommodations have implemented innovative strategies to become more environmentally and socially sustainable, elevating the guest experience in the process. Here's how to identify a hotel truly committed to doing its bit for the planet.

It has a sustainability policy

A hotel committed to sustainability will typically have a sustainability policy on its website. This will spell out if it has been certified by a credible organisation such as EarthCheck or Leadership in Energy and Environmental Design (LEED) and flag specific sustainability initiatives it has implemented. If you can't find this information online, contact the hotel. If staff can't provide specifics, be wary. Bear in mind, however, that smaller hotels often struggle to afford the often expensive improvements required to meet certification criteria, so don't be too quick to judge accommodation providers on that basis alone.

It's locally owned and run

While many international hotel chains now have admirable sustainability policies, opting for a local-owned and run lodging means your tourist dollars directly support the local community. In regions where accommodation providers have yet to adopt sustainable practices, a local guesthouse is still a more sustainable choice than a big foreign-owned hotel.

It's committed to limiting its environmental impact

Hotels that have had sustainability at heart from conception are generally more low-impact, but many older hotels have done a commendable job of greening up their act. Beyond the implementation of energy- and water-conserving technologies.

ECO HOTELS

72% of global travellers surveyed for Booking.com's 2019 Sustainable Travel Report said they weren't aware of the existence of eco-labels for holiday accommodations.

GREEN HOTEL BOOKING SITES

The sustainable travel movement has given rise to hotel booking websites specialising in ecofriendly properties. These industry leaders help do away with the guesswork when you're trying to book a sustainable stay.

★ **Ecobnb:** Find sustainable B&Bs in more than 30 countries. www.ecobnb.com
★ **Fairbnb:** Book local-owned accommodation in Europe and help fund community projects. www.fairbnb.coop
★ **Green Pearls:** Discover stunning sustainable hotels around the world. www.greenpearls.com
★ **BookDifferent:** Choose from more than two million green accommodations worldwide. www.bookdifferent.com

initiatives to look out for include an on-site produce garden that supplies the hotel restaurant, rooftop beehives, single-use-plastic-free amenities, locally made furnishings, recycling bins in guest rooms, the use of ecofriendly cleaning products, and washing linens only on request.

It works closely with the local community

Sustainable hotels empower local communities. This usually takes the form of hiring local staff (at fair rates, and with opportunities for career progression), using local suppliers, supporting sustainable community programmes, and integrating guests with the community on the community's terms, for instance via local-run tours that support the area's businesses and encourage the preservation of cultural traditions.

It encourages guests to get involved

A truly sustainable hotel will inspire guests to leave the destination in a better condition than they found it. This might entail interactive initiatives such as providing reusable water bottles and/or filtered water refills, free or cheap bicycle rental or shared transport options, guest experiences that support local people and businesses, incentives for guests who arrive by public transport or opt out of having their room serviced, and hosting environmental clean-up events. Sustainable hotels also typically encourage guests to support their mission face to face at check-in.

THE RISE OF CARBON-NEUTRAL HOTELS

The most climate-friendly hotel is a carbon-neutral hotel. The greenest examples carbon-offset the lowest percentage of emissions, which means they generate more of their own (renewable) power. Due to open in 2021, Svart hotel in the Norwegian Arctic is promising to be the world's first energy-positive hotel, designed to harness geothermal and solar energy to produce a surplus of solar power that can be redirected back to the grid. www.svart.no

How to choose a sustainable volunteering project

From installing healthy cook stoves in remote Peruvian villages to collecting data on vulnerable African wildlife, volunteering can be a rewarding way to spend time away. The UN considers volunteerism indispensable to achieving its Sustainable Development Goals – but some volunteer-abroad programmes are more sustainable than others.

© CRAIG LOVELL / EAGLE VISIONS PHOTOGRAPHY / ALAMY STOCK PHOTO

'To get the most out of volunteering you need to put effort into choosing who you go with and what you do', says Dr Kate Simpson, an expert advisor in Lonely Planet's Volunteer: A Traveller's Guide to Making a Difference Around the World who has spent years researching and working in the international volunteering industry. The following questions are designed to help you learn as much as possible about the quality, value and sustainability of volunteer projects before you dedicate your time to a particular one.

What work will I be doing?

An organisation with a good volunteer programme should be able to tell you what sort of work you will be doing, including how many hours a day and how many days a week, and with which host organisation, well in advance of the project start date. A typical source of dissatisfaction for volunteers is not doing what they planned (and paid) to do.

Does the organisation work with a local partner organisation?

If a volunteer programme is to be of value to a local community it should work in collaboration with, rather than be imposed on, that community. Find out who that partner is and how the relationship works. Is someone from the local organisation involved in the day-to-day management of your project? What sort of local consultation took place to build the project? Why is the project valuable?

What time frame is the volunteer programme run on?

A well-structured volunteer programme should have a clear time frame, and organisations should know from one year to the next whether a programme will continue. One-off programmes, and especially placements, can be problematic. If you are acting as a teaching assistant for a month, what happens the rest of the school year? Are other volunteers sent or is the arrangement simply ended? It may also be very disruptive for children to have a constantly changing staff. Establishing the level of commitment an organisation has to a given project or placement is vital in determining the quality, and therefore value, of that volunteer programme.

Does the organisation have policies to safeguard locals, wildlife and the environment?

All volunteer organisations should have a safeguarding policy for children and vulnerable adults whether they work with them or not, and programmes that work directly with children must include child protection training for volunteers. Similarly, high-welfare wildlife sanctuaries have policies to protect wildlife (restrictions on human-animal

WHY DO YOU WANT TO VOLUNTEER?

Don't forget to analyse your intentions for volunteering. Do you legitimately want to give back to the less fortunate, or, truth be told, are you more interested in seeking validation from your peers on social media, or using the experience as career leverage? If you approach volunteering with the curiosity and humility to learn, you – and the project – will get much more out of it.

contact are common), with appropriate training provided to volunteers. A volunteer organisation should also be able to tell you how it works to minimise the environmental footprint of its programmes.

What support and training will you receive?

Learning about both the practicalities of your volunteer job and the culture of where you are travelling to will help you get and give the most. Organisations offer vastly different levels of training and support. Look for one that provides not only pre-departure

training but also in-country support and guidance. Local support is also important, but ask if 'local' means just across the road or several hours away by bus. Make sure there is somebody in the country with direct responsibility for you. All projects require problem-solving at some point – you will need someone on hand to assist you with this.

Does the organisation make any financial contributions to its volunteer programmes? If so, how much?

Volunteer programmes need funds as well as labour, so ask how the cost of your placement is spent, and be persistent about getting a clear figure, not a percentage of profits. Also, be aware that payments for your food and lodging often do not assist your volunteer programme.

ECO-HACK

The ChildSafe Movement website, powered by child-focused NGO Friends International, is a helpful resource for travellers interested in volunteering with children. www.thinkchildsafe.org

Essential items for your zero-waste travel kit

There's more to minimising waste on the road than avoiding single-use plastic. Help reduce your impact across the board by making the following items your new travel essentials.

1 REUSABLE WATER BOTTLE

If you're travelling to a destination that is going to be lacking clean drinking water, bring water purification tablets or a Steripen (www.steripen.com), or upgrade to a bottle with a built-in filter like a LifeStraw (www.lifestraw.com).

2 REUSABLE COFFEE CUP

Particularly useful for air travel – simply ask the cabin crew to fill your own cup instead of a disposable one.

3 REUSABLE CUTLERY/TUPPERWARE

These come in handy when eating at street stalls (just ask the vendor to serve your meal in your own container) and for storing travel snacks.

4 PLASTIC-FREE TOILETRIES

Consider making your own products (for more on how to do this, flip over to p34), and upgrade your toothbrush, razor and hairbrush to sustainable plastic-free models when they next need to be replaced.

5 REUSABLE TOTE BAG

Given cotton is water- and-chemical intensive to grow, reach for a bag made out of recycled PET plastic, which is light and strong.

6 SMALL CLEAR TOILETRIES BAG

Use this for carrying liquids in hand luggage, instead of reaching for a zip-lock plastic bag at the airport, which you won't be able to reuse as many times.

8   FEMININE HYGIENE ALTERNATIVE

Not keen on menstrual cups? Consider period panties made by the likes of Modibodi. www.modibodi.com

9   PLASTIC-FREE SMARTPHONE CASE

Protect your phone with a compostable case and screen protector made by the likes of Pela. www.pelacase.com

10   USB/SOLAR-RECHARGEABLE DEVICE

Travel essentials like head torches are now available in rechargeable models, negating the need for batteries, while a solar device charger will help to reduce your impact on the local power supply (especially handy at wilderness camps that have a limited power supply).

ECO-HACK

Instead of using plastic bags to separate dirty clothes and shoes in your suitcase, invest in packing cubes, which you can wash between trips.

7   SCRUBBA

Looking like a dry bag, this clever Australian invention acts as a portable washing machine: it cleans clothes effectively and saves water. www.thescrubba.com.au

...AND THREE WASTEFUL PRODUCTS YOU CAN LOSE FROM YOUR TRAVEL KIT

★ **Wet wipes:** Opt for a biodegradable alternative if you can't live without them, but still don't ever bury or flush them.
★ **Mini toiletries:** At the very least, reuse the containers.
★ **Disposable in-flight amenity kits:** Invest in a reusable sleep mask so you won't have to reach for a low-quality alternative.

DIY plastic-free toiletries

ECO-HACK

Coconut oil is hydrophobic – meaning it repels water – so when applied as a pre-wash conditioner, it inhibits the penetration of water into each strand, making it less prone to damage and breakage.

Toiletries are one of the biggest sources of disposable plastics you're likely to encounter on the road. A greener and cheaper method is to make travel essentials yourself. Kate Nelson, the plastic-free activist behind the I Quit Plastics book and website (www.iquitplastics.com) and @plasticfreemermaid Instagram handle, shares her top recipes below.

DEODORANT

Coconut oil melts in warm climates, so use less of it in summer as the mixture will be easier to apply (with your finger or a small spoon).

Ingredients

★ 3 tbsp cold-pressed coconut oil
★ 2 tbsp arrowroot powder
★ 1 tbsp bicarb (baking) soda
★ A few drops of essential oil (geranium or lotus flower work well)

SHAMPOO

Bicarb (baking) soda removes dirt and build-up from the scalp, though as it can dry out the hair over time, you could a coconut oil treatment to your routine.

Ingredients

★ ¼ cup bicarb (baking) soda
★ A few drops of essential oil (lemon for blonde, rosemary for brunette, camomile for shine and strength)
★ 1 cup water

CONDITIONER

This simple recipe adds body while helping to regulate the scalp's pH balance – helpful as the pH level of the bicarb (baking) soda in your own-made shampoo is quite high.

Ingredients

★ 1 tbsp apple cider vinegar
★ 1 cup water

INSECT REPELLANT

Simply concocted from oil and wax, this ointment uses essential oils whose insect-repellant qualities have been exploited for centuries. It stays on the skin, making a protective barrier.

Ingredients
★ 5 tbsp almond oil
★ 5 tbsp coconut oil
★ 1 drop eucalyptus oil
★ 2 drops tea tree oil
★ ½ tsp lemon juice
★ 1 tbsp beeswax

Method
★ Double boil the almond oil, coconut oil and beeswax.
★ Stir in the lemon juice while still on the heat so the beeswax doesn't harden.
★ Pour into small clean jars.
★ Add essential oils (adding while on the heat will cause them to evaporate), stir quickly with a toothpick, and close the lid.

TOOTHPASTE

This product is best stored in the fridge but is fine to leave out while travelling. Just try not to get water in it, as that can make the mixture ferment.

Ingredients
★ ¼ cup coconut oil
★ ¼ cup bicarb (baking) soda
★ 15–20 drops peppermint oil

BODY MOISTURISER

Oil is not moisturising on its own, but it can help to trap moisture, so massage it into your body when you're in the shower and then wipe off the water and oil with a towel. Reach for cooling coconut oil in hot weather and warming black sesame oil in colder weather.

FACE MOISTURISER

Apply your essential oil of choice (rosehip is full of antioxidants) right after showering. For cool-climate trips, you may wish to craft a homemade balm that consists of one part melted beeswax (or cacao butter) and two parts essential oil.

MAKE-UP REMOVER

Wash your face with a warm wet washcloth, then apply essential oil (the same one you use for moisturising) to your face in small gentle circles with fingers, then wipe off with a warm wet washcloth. Do your eyes last if you're wearing heavy make-up.

How sustainable is your travel gear?

Accounting for a whopping 10% of global emissions, the textile industry is the world's second-biggest industrial polluter, behind oil. Sustainable adventure-wear pioneer Patagonia (www.patagonia.com) has made products from recycled plastic bottles since 1993, followed by other travel gear companies. But with greenwashing still rife in the industry, it pays to research brands before picking up new gear.

ECO-HACK

The world's first online retailer dedicated to sustainable travel clothing and kit, the Sustainable Travel Store is a handy one-stop-shop for your eco-travel needs. Currently it only ships to the US but may expand in future. www.sustainabletravelstore.com

How to tell if a travel gear company is sustainable

Ultra-sustainable companies tick most – if not all – of the following boxes.

★ Makes long-lasting, high-quality products.
★ Uses natural, sustainable, and recycled materials in their products, with as little chemical intervention as possible.
★ Lists a comprehensive sustainability policy on its website that is transparent about where and how its products are made.
★ Uses ecofriendly packaging for online purchases.
★ Offers a comprehensive warranty on all goods.
★ Offers a gear repair service.
★ Gives back via environmental or social initiatives such as 1% for the Planet (www.onepercentfortheplanet.org).
★ Is listed in ethical fashion directories such as Good on You (www.goodonyou.eco).
★ Is a certified B Corporation (a business that meets the highest standards of verified social and environmental performance), or is striving to become one.

The best fabrics for the environment

★ **Remember:** just because a fibre can be cultivated sustainably doesn't always mean it is manufactured sustainably.

★ **Tencel:** A brand name for a type of lyocell – a super-breathable fibre made from sustainably harvested wood pulp that has been embraced by the travel gear industry – Tencel is produced via a closed loop process, meaning the solvents used to turn the pulp into fibre are recycled over and over again.

★ **Hemp:** Incredibly easy on the Earth, producing up to double the yield of cotton per hectare, this natural fibre can be turned into fabric sustainably, though be mindful that some manufacturers do use chemicals.

ECO-HACK

Perfect for use at home and at laundrettes while travelling, the GuppyFriend washing bag traps nasty microfibres so you can dispose of them thoughtfully rather than letting them wash down the drain.
www.guppyfriend.com

★ **Bamboo:** While bamboo is one of the most sustainable crops to grow, note that the cheaper and more popular method used to turn it into the soft, wrinkle-free fabric that makes it so perfect for travelling is chemical-intensive.

The worst fabrics for the environment

While 'high-performance' fabrics are often great for travel, manufacturers either embed chemicals in the yarn or apply finishes or coatings after production, which can be hazardous to the environment, and maybe also to human health.

★ **Cotton:** While cotton is a natural, biodegradable fibre, it is also one of the most environmentally demanding crops – organic cotton uses even more water during the first one or two crop rotation cycles.

★ **Synthetics:** Fabrics like polyester, nylon, rayon and acrylic are usually produced from oil, meaning they are dependent on fossil fuel extraction. They also shed harmful microfibres into waterways.

★ **Animal-derived materials:** The leather and fur industries are responsible for huge methane outputs, with strong chemicals typically used to treat the goods. While wool is a renewable resource, the industry is behind vast swathes of land clearing and, like cows, sheep produce a high volume of methane.

© KEN ETZEL / PATAGONIA

10 GREAT ECO-TRAVEL APPS

ECO-HACK

Assert your right to online privacy and ensure you can access the websites and apps you'll need while travelling by downloading a trusted virtual private network (VPN) before you hit the road.

Smartphones may not be smart for the planet, but you can mitigate the impact of owning one by loading apps that help you travel more responsibly and sustainably.

1 TripCase
www.tripcase.com

A digital repository for important travel information: forward booking confirmations to TripCase's email address and it populates the details in your account.

2 Maps.Me
www.maps.me

Dispense with hard copies or wi-fi hunting by downloading offline destination maps. Maps.Me marks more hiking trails than the similar Google Maps function.

3 Citymapper
www.citymapper.com

Catching public transport abroad is a breeze with this real-time transit planning app, now available in 40 global cities.

4 Spinlister
www.spinlister.com

Like Airbnb for sports equipment, letting you rent bicycles, surfboards, stand-up paddleboards, skis and snowboards while you're away.

5 Duolingo
www.duolingo.com

Brush up on key phrases in the language of your proposed destination to help you connect more clearly and meaningfully with locals.

6 Abbyy Business Card Reader
www.abbyybcr.com

Save paper by scanning cards for hotels, tour guides and other contacts, for easy reference later.

7 Tipster

Nail tipping etiquette abroad with this quick reference guide to tipping for various services.

8 The Stop App
www.stopthetraffik.org/stopapp

Spotted something fishy? Report suspected incidents of human trafficking to UK-based not-for-profit Stop The Traffik.

9 Good Guide
www.goodguide.com

Run out of some essentials en route? This app provides sustainability ratings for more than 75,000 personal care and household products.

10 iOverlander
www.ioverlander.com

Made by overlanders for overlanders, pinpointing everything from campsites to mechanics and embassies on popular overlanding routes.

Pre-trip checklist for a sustainable journey

Prep for a responsible trip and reduce the energy footprint you leave behind by ticking these things off your to-do list before you depart.

Within three months of departure

★ Get the travel immunisations recommended by your doctor
★ Book the appropriate travel insurance for the destination and activities you plan to do, which may require add-ons to a standard policy
★ Cancel or suspend magazine subscriptions and food deliveries
★ Check if you can opt to receive any of your regular mail electronically instead

Within a week of departure

★ Save your travel booking confirmations as PDFs on your smartphone for easy offline access unless it's absolutely necessary to print them
★ Load up your smartphone with apps to help you tread lightly in your destination (flip to p38 for a list of the best contenders).
★ If flying, save paper by checking in online
★ Clean out uneaten food in your fridge to improve its energy efficiency

On the day of departure

★ Pack plastic-free snacks for the journey, and don't forget your zero-waste kit (see p32 for more on this).
★ Unplug all appliances in your home that don't need to stay on as devices drain power even when turned off
★ Rather than leave a light on to deter thieves, use a timer or check if there is an app you can download to turn lights on remotely every now and then
★ If you need to leave a thermostat on to prevent pipes freezing, set it to the lowest temperature possible and use timers
★ If travelling in summer, think about turning off the hot water heater
★ Consider taking public transport to your point of departure

---

HOW TO PACK LIGHTER EVERY TIME

★ Invest in a compact lightweight suitcase
★ Decant liquid toiletries into smaller reusable containers
★ Use the KonMari Method to fold your clothes (www.konmari.com)
★ Empty clutter out of your wallet and handbag or daypack
★ Switch hefty books for an e-reader
★ Leave heavy hair tools at home
★ Pack by outfit, rather than bringing individual garments that may not work together
★ Lay everything out before you pack and assess if you really need everything

---

ON THE ROAD

13 ways to reduce your carbon emissions when you travel

With the travel industry responsible for 8% of total global emissions, every action you take to curb your carbon is worthwhile.

1) FLY SMART

If you fly, reduce in-flight emissions by choosing a carbon-efficient airline, a direct flight and a seat in economy (coach) class instead of business. Other tactics include lowering window shades (to help keep the plane cool), bringing your own amenities and food (or, failing that, pre-ordering a plant-based meal).

2) PACK LIGHT

No matter what type of transport you'll be taking to reach your destination, or once you get there, a lighter suitcase requires less energy to transport.

3) UTILISE PUBLIC TRANSPORT

Taking public transport (or even better, a cycle rickshaw) won't only help to reduce emissions, but you'll also tick off a classic local experience. Many global cities are now equipped with affordable bike-, e-bike or scooter-share facilities.

4) USE ELECTRIC VEHICLES OR E-TAXIS

Electric vehicle (EV) infrastructure is improving around the world ever year (for EV road trip inspiration, see p82). And while major ride-share apps Uber and Lyft have yet to introduce EV-booking systems, both companies are currently incentivising drivers to make the switch over to electric vehicles.

5) SLEEP GREEN

Low-carbon hotels generally run on renewable energy, use energy-saving lights and other appliances, recover rainwater, recycle and use local products (see p28 for more info on choosing a green hotel). Slash more emissions by foregoing housekeeping and minimising your electricity and water usage.

6) CHOOSE LOW-CARBON ACTIVITIES

From walking and cycling tours to non-motorised snorkelling and diving excursions, carbon-light activities are better for your health as well as the health of the planet.

7 SKIP THE TOURIST TAT

Typical tourist souvenirs create a triple emissions whammy: they're made from plastic or chemically modified fabrics, in emissions-belching factories, and are transported in gas-guzzling trucks, ships or planes. For tips on sustainable souvenirs, see p60.

see p60.

ECO-HACK

Several subscription-based apps offer a one-stop-shop approach to carbon offsetting. Wren (https://projectwren.com) calculates a monthly offset fee based on your lifestyle (including travel); you can choose which carbon-reducing project to donate the cash to each month.

8 EAT LOCAL

Sampling regional delicacies at local-run stalls and restaurants is one of the great joys of travel, and choosing foods that are grown and produced locally helps to reduce food miles (emissions created by transporting food). Small farms are also more likely to adopt ecofriendly practices like avoiding of toxic pesticides – ask for info before you buy.

11 SKIP THE LONG SHOWERS

From Cape Town to Kathmandu, many travel hotspots around the world struggle with water shortages. By using less water, we can not only help to reduce pressure on the local water supply, but also help to slash the emissions created by treating and pumping water.

9 EAT LESS MEAT

With greenhouse gas emissions from agribusiness on track to surpass that of all other sectors, including energy, transport and industry, the single best way of reducing emissions on the road (aside from not flying) is to lower your intake of meat, particularly red meat, which creates the most livestock emissions.

12 CARBON-OFFSET ALL JOURNEYS

Planes aren't the only form of transport that spew out carbon. US-based offCents (www.offcents.com) tracks and offsets car, train and plane trips, while Swiss non-profit MyClimate (www.myclimate.org) also offsets car journeys, cruises, events and more.

10 EMBRACE ZERO-WASTE TRAVEL

Every product you use on your trip requires energy to manufacture, more energy to recycle, and releases emissions when it breaks down. By curbing waste whenever possible, you'll also curb emissions.

13 LINE-DRY YOUR TRAVEL CLOTHES

There's not always time to line-dry travel gear when you're on the move, but with one dryer load using five times more electricity than washing, it's worth packing a travel clothes line to use when you can.

How to nail single-use plastic-free travel

Plastic's devastating effect on the environment is making ever bigger headlines, yet our pledge of plastic-free living is often forgotten on holiday when we can be susceptible to the temptations of convenience and ease. Here's how to stay on track.

Embrace your zero-waste travel kit

By investing in zero-waste products you love (see p32 for tips on this) and keeping them in your handbag or daypack at all times, you'll never get caught out having to settle for single-use coffee cups, disposable plastic bags and eating utensils, single-use plastic bottles and more.

Be prepared to purify water anywhere

A lack of clean drinking water in your destination is no longer an excuse to rely on single-use plastic bottles. There are now loads of water purification options available to travellers, from filtration bottles such as the LifeStraw Go (www.lifestraw.com), which can filter five years' worth of clean water, to the Steripen (www.steripen.com), which uses ultraviolet rays to zap the nasties in 1L of water in 90 seconds. Meanwhile, the taste of water-purification tablets can also be easily masked by vitamin C effervescent tablets.

Sidestep in-flight plastic

Most airlines still use an outrageous amount of single-use plastics during in-flight

services. Help reduce your flight's contribution to landfill by asking the cabin crew to refill your reusable bottle during the drinks service, and consider refusing plastic-wrapped refresher towels, sweets, blankets, headphones and amenity kits. Should you forget your reusable bottle or cup, hang on to the same cup for the duration of the flight.

Opt for ecofriendly accommodation

Hotels committed to lowering their environmental impact (see p28) make it easier for you to avoid single-use plastic by providing water-bottle refills instead of single-use bottles, alternatives to plastic straws at the bar, bathroom amenities in reusable dispensers, and other single-use plastic swaps.

ECO-HACK

Make it easier for others to travel single-use plastic-free by starting conversations about plastic with local businesses. The owners might not even be aware of the environmental benefits of switching common plastics for lower impact alternatives.

Choose ecofriendly activity operators

Before you book an excursion in your destination, ask how drinks and meals will be served. Mindful companies offer water-bottle refills instead of single-use plastic bottles, and serve meals with reusable utensils rather than disposable plastic or polystyrene versions. Learn more about choosing a responsible operator on p26.

Be a savvy diner

A bit of forward-planning can make all the difference when it comes to drinking and dining on the road. Before ordering drinks at a new bar or restaurant, check that your tipple of choice doesn't come from a plastic bottle, and always request it sans straw. When it comes to street food, hand your reusable container to the vendor before they automatically serve your meal in a plastic container.

Shop at markets

Supermarkets are notorious for using unnecessary plastic packaging. Avoid it by shopping for food at fresh produce markets. The same goes for handicrafts – buying locally made, plastic-free goods saves on the plastic packaging typically used in transportation, and on the carbon impact of importing goods. But wherever you shop, don't forget to bring your reusable carrier bags!

How to harness culinary tourism for good

Offering a delicious insight into local traditions, food is an integral part of travel. When managed sustainably, culinary tourism can also forge cross-cultural connections, preserve local heritage and create sustainable economic opportunities for locals.

To be a sustainable diner is to consider all factors that come into play with the food we eat: where it comes from, how it was produced, what it's packaged in and the working practices of the establishment or vendor serving it. This level of information isn't always easy to come by when you're travelling, but by making an effort to seek out socially progressive and environmentally conscious places to eat, you can feel good about tucking in.

Dine in sustainable restaurants

Many restaurants have integrated sustainability practices such as committing to serve sustainably sourced, local, home-grown and organic produce; implementing procedures to reduce waste; and supporting sustainable community initiatives. By choosing to dine at these places, not only do you reward them for choosing to promote sustainability, but you also encourage others to join the movement.

Choose local, in-season dishes

Fresh local produce not only tastes better, it helps to support local farmers, requires less energy to store and motivates chefs to get creative. If you're not sure what's local or in season, ask your server. A sustainable seafood app like Seafood Watch (www. seafoodwatch.org) can also be helpful for doing your own research.

Try the vegetarian option

With the meat industry – particularly red meat – responsible for more than 14% of global emissions, you can help to limit your contribution by eating veggie or vegan more. HappyCow (www.happycow. net) is handy for locating plant-based restaurants and grocery stores in more than 180 countries.

Order only what you can finish

Instead of ordering several courses at once, start with one and add more until you're full. The same goes for buffets – only load up your plate with as much food as you're prepared to finish. With some buffet restaurants offering discounts to diners who clean their plates, this strategy could also save you money.

Don't be afraid to request dish modifications

It doesn't hurt to enquire whether the chef can accommodate any specific requests – if a smaller serving of rice or leaving out a vegetable you dislike means you'll be more likely to finish the dish and reduce food waste, go ahead and ask.

Put your zero-waste kit to use

A reusable food storage container and cutlery are perfect for street-food dining; if you forget to bring them along, wipe clean any disposable cutlery you're given and reuse them another time.

Segregate food waste properly

Rather than dumping fast-food packaging into the nearest landfill bin, ask around about recycling facilities. Or consider 'packing it out' – one of the principles of the Leave no Trace movement – to the next destination that has them.

Social dining apps to try on your next trip

Having trouble finding authentic eats in your destination? Allow a local to cook you your dinner instead.

Eatwith: Book meals, food tours and other culinary experiences run by locals in more than 130 countries. www.eatwith.com

Traveling Spoon: Consider adding a cooking class or market visit to a home-cooked meal booking. www.travelingspoon.com

ChefsFeed: The reincarnation of the Feastly app connects diners with food experiences run by chefs across the US. www.chefsfeed.com

Cheap food!

Help to minimise food waste while scoring a free or discounted meal with these apps.

Too Good to Go: Snap up discounted unsold food from shops and restaurants in 13 European countries. www.toogoodtogo.com

Olio: Connect with neighbours and local shops around the world that are keen to give away unwanted food. Simply update your 'home' location when travelling. www.olioex.com

Food For All: Pick up a takeaway meal for at least 50% off from restaurants in New York and Boston which have a surplus before they close for the day. www.foodforall.com

Karma: Eat out for less with the Karma app, which connects customers with restaurants in the UK, Sweden and France offering discounted surplus food. www.karma.life

FOOD PRODUCTS TO AVOID WHEN TRAVELLING

Sampling new foods is one of the great joys of travelling. But keep in mind that cultural culinary traditions are not automatic markers of sustainability.

★ **Civet coffee:** Also known as kopi luwak, this luxury coffee is produced from coffee beans excreted by civets (wild cat-like mammals) in captivity.

★ **Foie gras:** The French delicacy (which will be banned in New York by 2022) is made from the enlarged livers of ducks and geese force-fed via a feeding tube.

★ **Bushmeat:** This meat (typically sold at local markets) is usually harvested illegally, often from endangered species.

★ **Snake wine:** The Southeast Asian elixir is typically made by drowning a live snake in a bottle of alcohol.

★ **Traditional Chinese medicines:** Many concoctions are made from the body parts of animals the TCM industry has aided in driving to the brink of extinction.

★ **Exotic delicacies:** Novelty dishes such as whale or shark fin soup are often harvested illegally. Even when a dish is legal to serve in that particular country, the methods of production tend to be cruel.

© SUTIPORN SOMNAM / GETTY IMAGES

Six tips for more sustainable wildlife holidays

As the dark truths behind many wildlife tourism activities come to light, the case for choosing more responsible options has never been stronger. Before making decisions, it's important to get your head around what responsible wildlife tourism means.

'The important thing to keep in mind is that wild animals are not entertainers', says Ben Pearson, Senior Campaign Manager for the Australian branch of international animal welfare non-profit World Animal Protection (www.worldanimalprotection.org). 'If you want to see wildlife on holiday, the best thing you can do is to find somewhere to see it in the wild', he adds. 'The next best option is seeking out a legitimate sanctuary that offers observation only, so the animals are free to display their natural behaviours.'

This might sound restrictive, but there's no better wildlife experience than one where the animals involved are as comfortable to be in your presence as you are happy to be in theirs. Follow these tips to ensure you don't upset the balance.

Keep your distance

'If a tourism venue offers the opportunity to ride, touch or get a selfie with a wild animal, there's every chance that animal has been treated cruelly', says Pearson. Animal shows, elephant rides, captive dolphin swims and interacting with big cats are more widely publicised examples of tourism experiences that compromise animal welfare, but even seemingly harmless interactions like visiting a hedgehog cafe can have devastating impacts.

'Smaller animals do not cope

well with being handled by humans', says Pearson. 'Sloths used in the tourism industry, for example, typically die within six months of capture.'

The alternative? Walking and vehicle safaris led by experienced guides offer the thrill of observing wildlife, while keeping the animals – and you – safe.

Seek out genuine sanctuaries

Wildlife sanctuaries provide valuable opportunities to view and learn about species that are difficult to spot in the wild, but it pays to do your research to ensure the places you plan on visiting are operating in the true sense of the term. On top of a no-contact policy, legitimate sanctuaries should have adequate enclosures.

'Check if the animals have room to move and display natural behaviours', says Pearson. 'Is there protection from the weather and somewhere for them to get away from visitors?'

Resist the urge to feed wildlife

Despite your best intentions, feeding wildlife – even if it's with its natural food source in only small quantities – can do more harm than good.

'As a result of continued feeding, animals become dependent on humans for food, and can become aggressive', says Pearson. Feeding wildlife can also make animals sick and wreak havoc with their breeding and migrating patterns.

Beware of grey areas

Be mindful that so-called sustainable alternatives to problematic activities often have their own issues.

'Elephant washing is a big one', says Pearson. 'Many people believe this is a better alternative to riding, but allowing tourists to wash an elephant requires a high level of control over the animal. With mud used as sun protection, this constant washing can have a negative impact on their welfare.'

Avoid animal souvenirs

Shunning souvenirs made from wild animals is also part of being a responsible wildlife tourist. For more information on this topic, flip to p60.

Speak up

'Raising awareness of poor animal treatment is one of the best things you can do to stop it', says Pearson, who suggests respectfully raising the issue with the venue, and sharing

ECO-HACK

Learn about at-risk wildlife in your destination and report suspected wildlife trafficking via the Wildlife Witness app, developed by wildlife monitoring NGO Traffic. www.wildlifewitness.net

your experience with friends and family via social media.

'We know most people partake in wildlife tourism experiences because they love animals', says Pearson. 'If more people are aware of the impact on wildlife welfare before they book their trip, they're less likely to support cruel venues and partake in problematic activities.'

MUST-WATCH PRE-TRIP WILDLIFE DOCUMENTARIES

★ **Love & Bananas (2018):** The practice of keeping Asian elephants captive for tourism is examined in this film about the rescue of a pachyderm in Thailand.

★ **Blood Lions (2015):** The link between South Africa's fake lion sanctuaries and its canned hunting industry is exposed in this difficult-to-watch documentary.

★ **Blackfish (2013):** In revealing the plight of SeaWorld orca Tilikum, this gripping documentary shows the cruelty of keeping cetaceans in captivity.

How to be a low-impact hotel guest

Choosing a sustainable hotel is great first step, but the decisions you make after you check in can also help to lower your impact and support the hotel industry in reducing its emissions, which currently account for 1% of the global total.

Treat your hotel room like your own room
Avoid requesting clean towels and sheets unless absolutely necessary, keep showers short and remember to turn off the TV, lights and air-con when not in use.

Use the 'do not disturb sign'
Do you really need your room serviced? Unless you've run out of toilet paper or need a spill cleaned up, hang the 'do not disturb' sign when you head out for the day to ensure your linen won't be unnecessarily laundered.

Embrace ecofriendly incentives
Some hotels offer food and drink vouchers and other perks for opting out of having your room serviced or for arriving by public transport instead of a car. If there are rewards to be had, you may as well enjoy them.

Resist in-room single-use amenities
Just because the plastic water bottles, mini-toiletries and other disposable amenities in your hotel room are free doesn't mean they're guilt-free. BYO sustainable essentials to avoid reaching for single-use options.

ECO-HACK

Keeping your hotel curtains drawn shut during the day puts less pressure on the air-con, while closing them in the evening traps warm air, with less energy required to heat the room.

Dine local

If your hotel has a restaurant that showcases local (or better yet, home-grown) produce, show your support by eating in.

Engage with staff

Sustainable hotels create fair employment opportunities for local people. If you don't meet locals in a variety of roles at hotels that claim to be invested in the local community, ask management why.

Get involved

Accommodation providers invested in local communities connect guests with sustainable, local-run tours and may also run positive-impact activities like beach clean-ups.

Give back

Does your hotel support a local charity? Consider making a donation, or offering your services for free if you have a skill they may be able to use.

Reuse your pool towel

Save unnecessary laundering by taking your pool towel back to your room at the end of the day to reuse, if the hotel allows it.

Bring your own water bottle to the gym and spa

Hotel gyms and spas are notorious for single-use plastic cups. Bring your own bottle to avoid being caught out.

Research tipping etiquette

As difficult as it can be for non-tipping cultures to accept, housekeeping staff in countries with a low minimum wage (including the US) rely on their tips. Responsible tipping guides are easily found online.

Speak up

Perhaps you hung up your bath towels and housekeeping laundered them anyway, contravening the hotel's environmental policy. Or maybe the hotel bartender had an affinity for plastic straws. Raising your concerns with the manager may help to instigate change.

Share the win

Did you have an incredible experience (or otherwise) at a hotel? Tell your peers and write a fair online review to help other sustainable-minded travellers make informed decisions about the hotels they choose to support.

THE END OF SINGLE-USE TOILETRIES?

In 2019 the InterContinental Hotels Group, whose portfolio includes more than 5600 hotels and 843,000 rooms, became the latest major hotel chain to announce plans to replace single-use toiletries with bulk dispensers. Effective by 2021, the move will save the use of about 200 million miniature bottles per year.

Going local, for locals

Choosing tourism products that help sustain the local community may require more research and forward planning, but you'll be helping your hosts while enjoying a priceless local experience.

© SOLSTOCK / GETTY IMAGES

Tourism accounts for about one in ten jobs globally and, according to the World Travel and Tourism Council, can disproportionately benefit those less well off in society. With that powerful data in mind, there are many ways you can make a positive contribution while immersing yourself in local culture. Opting for homestays and local-run guesthouses over international hotel chains puts money directly into the pocket of the community. Eating in local-owned restaurants and buying locally made handicrafts helps to preserve indigenous culture and creates meaningful employment opportunities for locals. And if you need someone to show you around, choose a guide who lives in the area for unbeatable on-the-ground expertise.

GUIDED BY LOCALS

These websites connect travellers with small, independent companies or individual local experts to help you plan the perfect day in your destination.

★ **City Unscripted:** Book an alternative city tour of more than 40 global cities or design your own. www.cityunscripted.com

★ **Embark.org:** Choose your own outdoor adventure with adrenaline junkies around the world. www.embark.org

★ **Showaround:** Line up a local to show you around (sometimes for free) in a more informal style than a traditional guided tour. www.showaround.com

★ **ToursByLocals:** Browse itineraries in 159 countries designed by locals or work with them to create a bespoke private tour. www.toursbylocals.com

★ **Urban Adventures:** Book day tours designed and run by locals in 160 cities worldwide. www.urbanadventures.com

★ **Withlocals:** Choose from local-led tours in more than 40 cities across Asia, Europe and Africa, with an emphasis on food tours. www.withlocals.com

ECO-HACK

Designed to immerse travellers in local life beyond tourist centres, G Adventures' Living Locals tours are based in agriturismos, family homes, jungle homestays and even Mongolian gers (yurts). www.gadventures.com

Should you still visit places where locals don't want tourists?

From Barcelona to Dubrovnik, Venice to Santorini, some popular travel destinations have become so overwhelmed with tourists that locals have asked visitors to stay away. So should you? When it comes to places where tourism represents a major source of income, avoiding them altogether could have negative consequences for the local workforce. If you do decide to visit, aim to travel during the low season, support local businesses and choose accommodation options that don't have a direct negative impact on locals (which short-term apartment rentals in residential buildings have been blamed for).

The rise of agritourism

If you've spent the night in a converted dairy farm in the English countryside, taken selfies in a sunflower plantation in Australia or squished grapes between your toes in southern France, you've (perhaps unknowingly) taken part in agritourism. It's an industry that's expected to see continued growth as travellers seek to become more connected with the environment and the origins of products.

Whether it's an organic fruit and vegetable farm running a farm-gate cafe, a dairy farm inviting guests to milk cows, or a ranch converting idyllic unused land into space for temporary accommodation facilities, agritourism offers guests new insights and experiences while directly benefiting local farmers. These additional revenue streams can be fundamental for the continued success of small sustainable producers, which often face competition from industrial operations that are able to produce higher volumes at a lower cost via less sustainable farming methods. Fancy staying on to help out around the farm in exchange for room and board? Consider WWOOFing (www.wwoof.net).

PAY IT FORWARD

Leave a positive impact on communities you visit by supporting social enterprise businesses and other community initiatives. For more tips on how to give back while travelling, see p68.

The power of responsible indigenous tourism

Responsibly managed indigenous tourism provides a platform for meeting the world's first peoples in a meaningful way, leaving you with a fascinating insight into and a greater respect for the cultural heritage of your destination. In turn, your participation helps to keep the communities' arts, crafts and traditions alive for future generations.

From learning how Aboriginal Australians were guided by the dark spaces between the stars to practising the techniques used by the Inuit people of Canada to withstand Arctic winters, perhaps the best reason for experiencing indigenous tourism is the opportunity to learn from the ancient wisdom of the world's first peoples. Particularly poignant amid the climate crisis is the lesson you're bound to learn from any indigenous community you visit: we were not bequeathed the Earth, we are mere custodians looking after it for the next generation.

© EVANTRAVELS / SHUTTERSTOCK

© CLIQUEIMAGES / GETTY IMAGES

THE ART CODE

Up to 80% of 'Aboriginal art' marketed to tourists is thought to be fake, according to the Arts Law Centre of Australia. Avoid knock-offs by purchasing art directly from artists, or from established galleries affiliated with industry organisations such as the Indigenous Art Code. www.indigenousartcode.org

While indigenous tourism can greatly benefit the world's first peoples, not to mention help to promote cross-cultural understanding, it also has the potential to disrupt the delicate social balance of indigenous communities. As demand for indigenous tourism experiences continues to increase, it's essential to do your research to ensure that what you sign up for is truly respectful, and that indigenous groups are actually involved and will benefit from any operation.

In New Zealand, the national tourist board (www.newzealand.com) and Maori Tourism website (www.maoritourism.co.nz) both list a wealth of Maori-led tours. In Canada, the Aboriginal Tourism Association of Canada website (www.indigenouscanada.travel) lists three- to nine-day experiences, from village stays to arctic wildlife tours, all run by indigenous-owned businesses. In the vast state of Western Australia, the Western Australian Indigenous Tourism Operators Council (www.waitoc.com) is a great resource for Aboriginal tourism operators, while in northern Europe, the Swedish Lapland tourism website (www.swedishlapland.com), Norway tourism website (www.visitnorway.com) and Finland tourism website (www.visitfinland.com) are handy resources for learning about and booking Sámi tourism experiences in Lapland.

TIPS FOR RESPONSIBLE COMMUNITY VISITS

Choose a responsible operator: Responsible operators will be transparent about how the community they work with benefits, financially or otherwise. For tips on how to seek out responsible operators, see p26.

Ensure you're healthy: Care must be taken in areas where indigenous peoples' immunity to outside diseases may be poor. Even the common cold can be deadly.

Ask permission: The lands lived on or used by indigenous peoples should never be entered without their free and informed consent. Consent should also be obtained before taking photographs of people, their homes and sacred spaces.

Be respectful: Responsible tour operators provide etiquette briefings before community visits. If you don't receive one, ask for advice on appropriate conduct.

Reassess gift-giving: Distributing gifts to vulnerable children can be problematic. Instead, ask your tour operator in advance if the village needs certain supplies which you can hand over to an elder.

Pass on the school visit: Remember that children are not tourism attractions and that visits can disrupt valuable lesson time.

Buy handicrafts: Buying traditional art and handicrafts made by community members at fair prices ensures your money stays in the village, and supports creative traditions.

Pay fairly: Indigenous communities should be properly compensated for their services, which include welcoming you onto their land.

© HOMO COSMICOS / SHUTTERSTOCK

ECO-HACK

Visit indigenous sacred sites around the world respectfully by following the guidelines outlined by volunteer organisation Sacred Sites International Foundation. www.sacred-sites.org

In our increasingly high-tech world, it's not surprising that travellers are willing to pay for a glimpse of communities living more traditional lives. Unfortunately, many ethnic villages around the world have been exploited by tour operators looking for quick and easy profit. Travellers have contributed to this exploitation by viewing ethnic village visits as a photo opportunity rather than as a chance to genuinely engage with indigenous people and culture. Some 'hill tribe' villages in northern Thailand, for example, have been described as 'human zoos', where tribespeople are compelled to wear traditional clothing and pose for photos. The rise of so-called 'human safaris' designed to 'spot' reclusive indigenous tribes such as the Mascho-Piro of Peru is even more problematic. The 2018 death of American adventure blogger and missionary John Allen Chau at the hands of the isolated Sentinelese tribe he visited illegally in India's Andaman islands is just one example of the grave consequences of this form of ethnic tourism.

But ethnic village visits can be responsible and sustainable. In Namibia, a series of NGO-developed 'living museums' managed by San communities have created opportunities for Africa's first peoples to practise their culture through meaningful employment. Choose experiences wisely, and everybody wins.

UNSUSTAINABLE INDIGENOUS TOURISM EXPERIENCES TO AVOID

★ Village visits marketed as photo stops or shopping trips.

★ Performances by children when tips are expected.

★ Indigenous experiences guided by non-indigenous people for no clear reason.

SOURCE AUTHENTICITY

In 2018, representatives of Finland's indigenous Sámi urged holidaymakers to stop visiting igloos and riding husky sleds in Lapland, claiming non-Sámi traditions were being passed off as authentic, thereby exploiting their culture.

How to be a responsible travel photographer

'The moment you ask someone for a portrait, the interaction no longer becomes about what you want but about what they are willing to give you of themselves', says award-winning travel photographer Lola Akinmade Åkerström (pictured right). Here are her top tips for photographing people responsibly.

★ **Do your homework:** Learn the cultural norms and taboos of the place you're visiting when it comes to interacting with locals, particularly indigenous people. Respects starts before you even begin your trip.

★ **Ask permission:** Unless the person you are shooting is part of a broader photo story about a place, it's much more respectful to ask for their explicit permission. When it comes to photographing kids, seek a parent's or guardian's consent first.

★ **Say their name:** Proper acknowledgement should be the foundation of every exchange. Introduce yourself to people you wish to photograph and avoid sneaking shots if they will be the main subject of your photo.

★ **Appreciate their craft:** Show people that you appreciate what is important to them. Whether it's an artist or a fishmonger, spending time observing and even participating in their tasks communicates respect. Interactions also get you closer to your subjects, providing opportunities for strong photos.

★ **Smile:** A smile and gentle nod always go a long way and let your subject know that you are approachable. When photographing children, remember they love to be entertained – start with a big grin and go from there.

★ **Be patient:** Be open to learning about your subjects and their lives if you want to them to open up enough to give you a photo.

★ **Provide proper context:** What does their stance say? How are they posing? Are they standing proudly? Then try to capture

© MATT DUTILE / LONELY PLANET

often found that the way I hold my camera, with both hands and with the lens pointing downwards, in a submissive fashion, makes me less threatening and immediately puts the subject in the position of power in that momentary relationship. You can still exude confidence while showing humility.

and convey that in your image. Try to show more of your subjects' environment, too, which is part of their story.

★ **Change your disposition:** Getting a complete stranger to relax long enough to grant you momentary access into their world is one of the most difficult parts of travel photography. For me, I've

★ **Shift focus from one to many:** Especially when photographing children, try to shift your focus from the single child to the group. Even the most rambunctious and spirited kids get intimidated when cornered by an adult. Shifting focus away from one child to many, while 'focusing' on your main subject, can improve the atmosphere of your travel portrait.

★ **Elevate or shoot at eye level:** Always shoot at eye level or slightly below. On top of creating more intimate photos, this also creates an equal connection rather than 'looking down' at your subject.

★ **Buy something:** If the person you want to photograph is selling their craft or goods, buying something is a way of showing gratitude. Plus, the more you acknowledge people,

© MATT MUNRO / LONELY PLANET

RESPONSIBLE WILDLIFE PHOTOGRAPHY

Take it from the UK's Natural History Museum's prestigious Wildlife Photographer of the Year rulebook: portraying captive or restrained animals, or animals that have been baited, is banned. Not crowding wildlife, not using a flash when photographing nocturnal wildlife, and staying away from nests or dens (which can lead to abandonment by the parents) are also key to being a responsible wildlife photographer.

the less they see you as a stranger to whom they have no emotional connection.

★ **Keep your word:** If you made a promise either to send your subject a copy of their photograph or do something for them in return, keep your word. Properly thank people for their time, effort and energy, and show that you are trustworthy by delivering on your promises.

© JONATHAN GREGSON / LONELY PLANET

Sustainable souvenir shopping guide

Adapted from the French verb se souvenir (to remember), souvenirs are arguably best collected in the form of memories. But if you're partial to a holiday keepsake, or love to bring home gifts for family and friends, being a conscious consumer is key.

The global souvenir business is worth billions and provides vital income to local craftspeople. But as a largely unregulated industry, it's almost impossible to stop the surge of cheap imports that take business away from genuine artisans and wreak havoc on the environment due to their disposable nature. By approaching souvenir shopping as a way to support and learn about the communities you visit, you can do your bit to help locals while picking up items you'll regularly use and treasure for a long time to come.

Carefully chosen souvenirs made from environmentally friendly materials are a slice of the local culture that you can take home with you. Best of all, buying something made in the area supports artists and craftspeople and can provide an economic incentive to continue plying a trade or craft at risk of dying out – be it Kutnu silk weavings from Turkey, ceramic art in Uzbekistan or colourful woven kunaa mats from the Maldives.

Sustainable souvenirs to seek out

★ Sustainably produced and fairly priced artworks, textiles, clothing, jewellery and useful crafts, ideally purchased directly from the artisan. Aim for traditional over trend-based designs.

★ Plastic-free sustainable consumables – those bottles of Russian vodka and Italian truffle oil might not last long, but they're low-waste, and your family and friends won't love them any less.

★ Practical souvenirs made from recycled materials such as plastic bottles or paper, which encourages recycling.

★ Useful, sustainable souvenirs produced by local charitable organisations, so you know your money is going to a great cause.

★ Vintage clothing and other secondhand items, particularly from not-for-profit charity shops.

★ Ethical and sustainable fashion and homewares. Use the Good on You website or app (www.goodonyou.eco) to locate thousands of stores worldwide.

★ Look out for social-enterprise boutiques, which are businesses designed to provide sustainable employment to locals, and ultimately uplift communities. Choose products made from sustainable natural materials wherever possible.

★ Taking cooking classes abroad leaves you with recipes to share with family and friends back home.

© MATT MUNRO / LONELY PLANET

© MATT MUNRO / LONELY PLANET

ECO-HACK

Rather than have fragile travel buys packaged in bubble wrap and plastic-based tape, consider using a clean sock or perhaps a scarf to keep them safe instead.

Souvenirs to avoid

★ Jewellery and other products made from coral or seashells, both of which play an important role in the marine ecosystem. It may also be illegal to remove these products from the country, or bring them into your own.

★ Jewellery made from precious stones, unless their provenance can be proven via a legally valid certificate.

★ Items made from animal products, unless you can be 100% sure the products are environmentally sound and sourced sustainably. Do not take the vendor's word for it. Common items include tortoiseshell, bird feathers, mammal horns, furs and reptile skins.

★ Products linked to animal abuse such as civet coffee (also known as kopi luwak), snake wine, foie gras and Chinese medicines.

★ Unsustainable consumables such as caviar, which has pushed sturgeon fish to the brink of extinction.

★ Items made from endangered or limited resources such as exotic woods (like ebony and rosewood).

★ Cheap, mass-produced souvenirs such as novelty key rings and T-shirts. These are typically made from poor-quality unsustainable materials and produced offshore. The low-price points also threaten local craft industries.

★ Counterfeit goods. Production supports criminal industries, and the craftmanship rarely ever matches that of the original, meaning the products won't last as long.

★ Ancient artifacts. Not only does the purchase of these items fuel a market for procuring antiquities illegally, but most museums won't touch items you 'rescue' that don't have a spotless history.

★ Products from souvenir shops visited on mass-market-style tours. Chances are the tour operator will make a bigger commission than the artisan.

★ Anything sold by a child, which encourages child labour.

WHEN IN DOUBT...

★ Check labels for information on where the item was made and what it was made from.

★ When there's no label, ask questions. A seller with the right intentions will be happy to share this information.

★ Use your intuition: does the seller seem trustworthy? If it doesn't feel right, don't buy.

How to share your travels on social media more responsibly

Every social media user has the power to influence. Here's how to use that power for good.

'As more people look for travel inspiration online, what we post on social media matters', says Ellie Cleary, founder of responsible travel blog Soul Travel (www. soultravelblog.com). 'Social media platforms don't allow much room for context, so it's important to be aware of the ripple effect that posting your travel snaps can create.'

Help safeguard your destination – and also fellow travellers – by following these tips.

Tag the region, not the exact location

'When we geotag our social media posts, we don't always know what the consequences will be', says Cleary. Perhaps a poacher will use the information to locate and harvest an endangered rhino. Or maybe the post will draw an unsustainable surge of visitors to that out-of-the-way waterfall.

'Travel at its best has a bit of mystery, so help keep special places a little bit secret by tagging the region or country instead', suggests Cleary.

Avoid encouraging risky behaviour

Hundreds of travellers have lost their lives in pursuit of the perfect selfie, while many more have been injured or have landed themselves in serious trouble for disobeying local laws.

'While you might be a trained stunt artist, the average person scrolling through your photos or videos online is not, so social media users have a responsibility not to encourage our audiences to engage in unsafe behaviour', says Cleary. 'If you're set on posting a picture of something that not everyone could easily do, at least provide adequate context in the caption.'

Be mindful of cultural etiquette

Think hard before sharing a picture of yourself wearing a revealing outfit in a conservative or sacred place, or posing for a photo in a way that local people may find offensive, such as baring your behind.

'Posting culturally inappropriate travel snaps isn't just disrespectful to your destination hosts, but could also compromise the safety of your followers, such as setting up women for harassment', says Cleary. 'Instead, pay it forward by using social media to talk about things travellers need to be aware of before visiting the destination.'

Research the sustainability of tourism experiences

Posting a happy snap of yourself

on safari 'walking with' a captive lion or visiting a school might seem like innocent fun, but the negative impact of doing this can be huge.

'Posting pictures of cruel, unethical and potentially harmful tourism experiences gives them validity', says Cleary, who recommends using social media to call out attractions you have visited that weren't as ethical as they claimed to be.

Talk about responsible tourism on social media

Every social media user can be an ambassador for responsible tourism, says Cleary.

'Social media is the perfect forum to share responsible travel tips for the destinations you're posting about. Even if you only have 10 followers, that's 10 people you can engage in a conversation about how to make a difference in the places they visit.'

Choose your hashtags carefully

Hashtags help social media users filter relevant content, so using hashtags like #responsibletourism for any old travel post, rather than to showcase a particular tourism experience doing good, makes it difficult for people to understand what it means to travel responsibly.

'I only use responsible tourism-related hashtags when I feel that my post is relevant, such as a community project or an eco-lodge', says Cleary. 'That way people searching for responsible travel on hashtags will find the real deal.'

Collaborate wisely

Cleary believes that anyone using their digital influence to secure travel freebies or commercial collaborations has a duty to make sure they work with responsible

companies, and to be upfront about these relationships: 'When a company has paid for your post or has offered a product in exchange, you have an ethical responsibility (and in many countries, also a legal one) to disclose it – and that applies to everyone, not just users

ECO-HACK

Do you blog about your travels too? Consider joining the Responsible Travel Bloggers Facebook group (www.facebook.com/groups/responsibletravelbloggers) to pick up responsible blogging tips and connect with like-minded content creators.

© PETAR CHERNAEV / GETTY IMAGES

Keeping children safe

When we are confronted with children in vulnerable situations, the instinct to help can sometimes cloud our judgement. James Sutherland of Friends International, a social enterprise NGO focusing on children's empowerment, shares his advice on how to ensure the help you provide has a positive impact.

© KRIS DAVIDSON / LONELY PLANET

Child beggars

Developing economies are notorious for high numbers of beggars – especially children – in tourist areas. But Sutherland says handing out money or even just sweets to child beggars can lock them into a cycle of poverty.

'The reality is that giving handouts to child beggars does not help them out of the harmful situation they are in, in fact it keeps them there', says Sutherland. 'You give today, and tomorrow they will still be there, reaching out to someone else.'

Giving gifts to children

Even when children aren't begging, Sutherland says doling out gifts – even useful items such as pens and books – can also be problematic.

'Giving gifts to vulnerable children reinforces the traditional unsustainable "charity as handouts" approach and encourages children to interact in potentially harmful ways with travellers', says Sutherland.

HOW YOU CAN HELP KIDS WHILE TRAVELLING

Sutherland recommends seeking out organisations that are working to get children away from at-risk situations and supporting their efforts.

'These are often social enterprises that may run souvenir shops, training businesses or other initiatives such as income-generation projects for parents', says Sutherland. 'By supporting these you will help to break the cycles that lead children onto the streets and support them and their parents to have better, safer futures.'

© JUSTIN FOULKES / LONELY PLANET

© CRAIG LOVELL / EAGLE VISIONS PHOTOGRAPHY / ALAMY STOCK PHOTO

Child labour

Most travellers will encounter child labour in the form of kids selling anything from souvenirs to drinks.

'These children are often not attending school or are working in dangerous situations such as late at night', says Sutherland. 'Unfortunately they will remain in these situations if travellers continue to buy from them.'

Visiting orphanages and schools

While the issues involved with orphanage tourism are more widely known these days, the impact of school visits is not always considered.

'Ask yourself if you would do this at home', says Sutherland. 'The answer is invariably no, as it would disrupt classes.'

Volunteering with children

'Only professionals have access to vulnerable children at home, and that holds true for volunteering when you travel', says Sutherland. 'Even if you're a childcare professional, a more sustainable way to contribute is to share your skills with local staff rather than directly working with children.' For more information on volunteering with kids, see p32.

ECO-HACK

For more information on keeping children safe when you travel, check out the ChildSafe Movement website, powered by Friends International. www.thinkchildsafe.org

© JUSTIN FOULKES / LONELY PLANET

Navigating ethical dilemmas

On top of the dozens of decisions you'll face on the road every day, debating the ethics of certain situations or encounters can be overwhelming. Jeff Greenwald, Director of non-profit travel resource Ethical Traveler (www.ethicaltraveler.org), shares his insights on navigating common concerns more responsibly.

Haggling

'Be aware that haggling isn't always part of local culture', says Greenwald, who advises researching the item's value – and considering its value to you – before bargaining begins. 'The final price should leave both parties satisfied', he adds. 'Especially in places like Nepal or Morocco, where the profit margin can be very slim. Even if you overpay a little, it's better than leaving the vendor out of pocket.'

Tipping

Similarly to haggling, Greenwald advises travellers to be mindful that tipping can be considered rude or insulting in some cultures. And that over-tipping can have a ripple effect.

'Over-tipping can set an unrealistic standard for other travellers, and has the potential to upset the social balance', says Greenwald, adding that a tip of 10% is generally adequate. 'If tour guides start making more money than cardiac surgeons, as they do in places like Cuba, the temptation to work in tourism puts great pressure on essential services.'

Giving to beggars

While Greenwald does not recommend giving money or treats to children, he believes there are no clear-cut ethical guidelines when it comes to adult beggars.

'Begging comes in many forms – from religious to nuisance, from hardship to transactional, such as locals who offer to show you around for a tip', he says. 'While in some circumstances it may be wiser not to give, in the case of people with medical issues or alms seeking, it's entirely up to you to decide if you want to practise generosity.'

Paying for photos

Feel weird about paying for photos? You're not alone. But that doesn't mean it's unethical, unless the people asking for money are children.

'Some travellers feel that paying local people they photograph is inauthentic, but it's fair to expect that some may want to be remunerated for providing that service to you', says Greenwald. For more responsible travel photography tips, see p58.

Places with poor human rights records

Greenwald advises against visiting conflict zones but believes travelling to destinations behind the media curtain can be a force for good.

'Only by travelling to places ourselves can we truly understand them', he says. It can also be argued that travel boycotts punish society's most vulnerable.

'By supporting local businesses, witnessing how people live, and sharing their challenges and aspirations with a wider audience, travellers can help empower local people', Greenwald adds.

Slum tours

Slum tours raise all kinds of ethical concerns, from their potential to commodify poverty to the possibility that tours may help to fund crime. Yet some supporters counter that tours run by responsible residents can provide a valuable revenue stream for the community.

'It's important to do due diligence before signing up for any kind of community tour', says Greenwald. 'Be sure to ask how your money is distributed and be respectful of the people living there if you do visit.'

WHAT ABOUT THE ETHICS OF CERTAIN WILDLIFE TOURISM EXPERIENCES, YOU ASK?

Flip to p76 for tips on responsible safaris.

© PETER SEAWARD / LONELY PLANET

Nine ways to give back when you travel

Striving to leave the destinations you visit in a better state than you found them, to however small a degree, is part of being a responsible traveller. Here are a few ways to give something back.

1 PACK FOR A PURPOSE

Handing out pens and sweets to children on your travels might seem like a nice gesture, but this practice can inadvertently support a begging economy. Make gifting more meaningful by packing supplies most needed by schools, medical clinics and other community services in your destination as listed on the Pack for a Purpose website (www.packforapurpose.org). Simply drop off the supplies to the hotel or tour operator listed on the website, and they'll deliver the items on your behalf. This system helps to streamline deliveries and safeguard the welfare of local people.

2 TAKE A POSITIVE-IMPACT TOUR

A growing number of tour companies go a step further to support local people by building micro-volunteering activities into their itineraries. Perhaps you'll lend a hand microchipping wildlife while on safari in Africa, help install new cook stoves in a remote Peruvian village during a hike, or roll up your sleeves to clean enclosures at a wildlife sanctuary.

3 VOLUNTEER YOUR TIME OR SKILLS

If you're unable to commit to a longer project, ask your hotel or tour operator if there's a local initiative you might be able to get involved in during your visit. Perhaps an NGO could use your help setting up their social media account, the local dive centre is hosting a beach clean-up, or the town's animal shelter is short on dog walkers? For those with a whole day to spare, Give a Day Global (www.giveadayglobal.org) lists projects in 16 countries that could use your help.

4 DONATE TO A LOCAL NON-PROFIT

Got more money than time? Chances are there is a charity in your destination that would be grateful for a donation. Organisations like Global Giving (www.globalgiving.org) do the background checks for you, so you can be sure the contribution you wish to make will be going to a worthwhile cause.

5 SUPPORT WOMEN

Empowering women has been identified as key to combatting climate change. Make a concerted effort to support women on your travels by seeking out female tour guides, dining at female-owned restaurants and supporting female-owned businesses of all kinds.

ECO-HACK

Facebook's 'events' function can be helpful for locating opportunities to engage with and give back to the local community in your destination, from beach clean-ups to fundraising barbecues.

6 GIVE A MICROLOAN

Microloans help entrepreneurs in developing countries start or expand small businesses. Organisations like Kiva (www.kiva.org) do it all for you; simply browse for a project you'd like to support and choose how much you'd like to donate, from as little as US$25. As a condition of accepting the loan, the borrower must commit to repaying it over an agreed time period, allowing you to fund new loans or withdraw the money.

8 SUPPORT SUSTAINABLE BUSINESSES

Spend your tourist dollars at locally owned businesses rather than multinational chains. Look out for social enterprise businesses, which are specifically designed to improve the lives of local people. The Tree Alliance (www.tree-alliance.org), for example, runs seven excellent restaurants across Southeast Asia that act as vocational training centres for marginalised youth.

7 TAKE THREE FOR THE SEA

Treading lightly on your destination and making the effort to pick up litter, particularly on beaches and on wilderness trails, is one of the easiest ways to give back while travelling. Pledging to 'Take 3 for the Sea' (take3.org) helps clean up the local area, making it more pleasant for visitors and residents alike.

9 BE AN AMBASSADOR

Having the privilege to travel means you automatically become an honorary ambassador of your own country in the places you visit. And vice versa when you return. By serving in this capacity you can educate both sides, helping to break down barriers and trying to make the world a more peaceful place.

Embracing citizen science

Scientific environmental research needs enthusiastic volunteers: cue citizen science. This monitoring, measuring and recording of anything from movements of rare animals to washed-up marine flotsam helps scientists understand and protect our planet. And with many projects based in tourism areas, it's well suited to travellers.

A growing number of tour operators, particularly Antarctic expedition cruise companies, are integrating citizen science opportunities into their itineraries. Among the most common is a BioBlitz, where you can join scientists in finding and identifying as many species as possible in a designated area over a short period (usually 24 hours). But there are loads of other initiatives you can assist with as you traverse the globe, with little more than a smartphone and an internet connection required for most projects. Armchair travellers can even help from home, 'tagging' penguins in the Southern Ocean, for example, or scanning images of the night sky to help scientists learn more about 'clumpy' galaxies.

CITIZEN SCIENCE HOLIDAYS

The Earthwatch Institute runs worldwide citizen science expeditions that are designed and led by scientists, ranging from working with locals in Bali on combating plastic pollution to studying mammals in reforested areas of Brazil's Atlantic Forest. www.earthwatch.org

CITIZEN SCIENCE PROJECTS TO JOIN ON YOUR NEXT TRIP

ECO-HACK

Keen to create your own citizen science project? Bring it to reality with Zooniverse's comprehensive yet user-friendly Project Builder tool. www.zooniverse.org

Happy Whale
Upload photos of marine mammal encounters around the world to help scientists better understand population trends. www.happywhale.com

iNaturalist
Get this app to collect photos, share your observations on nature and discuss your findings. www.inaturalist.org

Globe at night
One for stargazers, this international citizen science project raises awareness of the effect of light pollution by inviting volunteers to measure night-sky brightness. www.globeatnight.org

Bumble Bee Watch
Learn about and help track North America's bumblebees to help researchers determine the status and conservation needs of these much-loved insects. www.bumblebeewatch.org

Penguin Watch
Penguin fan? Here's your chance to do your bit for conservation by helping to tag them online via this citizen science project on Zooniverse, the world's largest platform for people-powered research. www.zooniverse.org

eBird
Join the global effort to map bird ranges by sharing and logging sightings, photos and recordings on your travels. www.ebird.org

FrogID
Help save Australia's rapidly declining frog population by recording frog calls, finding a species match through the app and submitting your findings to the FrogID database. www.frogid.net.au

Journey North
Log your sightings of monarch butterflies, bald eagles, hummingbirds and more on their North American migration routes. www.journeynorth.org

Spider Spotter
Help European scientists learn how spiders adapt to city life by uploading pictures of the webs and arachnids you encounter. www.spiderspotter.com

Big Seaweed Search
Explore the UK coastline and record the living seaweeds you find via this Natural History Museum initiative, just one of several citizen scientist programmes the museum supports. www.nhm.ac.uk

Tips for responsible hiking

You might have heard of the 'Leave No Trace' principles, but there are many things to consider when planning a responsible wilderness hike anywhere in the world. Here are nine of the most important.

Plan it well

Doing the necessary preparation not only helps to keep you safe but also reduces pressure on local services. Pack for the appropriate weather conditions, bring sufficient food and water supplies, and tell someone where you're going and when to raise the alarm if you haven't checked in.

Hire a local guide

If you're setting out on a multi-day hike, hire a licensed local guide and/or porter. They will be well equipped to keep you safe and informed during the journey, and hiring local ensures your tourist dollars go straight back into the local community.

Carry it in, carry it out

What you bring on a hike should come back with you. This includes all food waste, toilet paper when you're unable to dig a hole and feminine hygiene products. On multi-day hikes with rubbish facilities (like teahouse treks in Nepal), consider how waste you leave en route might be disposed of – in most cases, it's more sustainable to pack it out.

Answer the call of nature responsibly

The Center for Outdoor Ethics in the US advises that number twos should be buried (with white, unbleached toilet paper only) in a hole 15 to 20cm deep and 60m from trails, camps and water sources. Trail too narrow? Pack out poo in a compostable bag secured in a 'poop tube' to dispose of responsibly later. The 60m rule also applies to a wild wee near a water source, but you needn't wander so far in dry areas.

Stick to marked trails

Hiking trails are designed to showcase the safest and most scenic route, while protecting natural

© STIAN KLO / LONELY PLANET

ECO-HACK

For solo hikes, long hikes, and hikes in areas with no phone service, consider carrying a personal locator beacon (PLB). Beacons should only be activated in a life-threatening situation.

habitats. Avoiding the urge to go rogue ensures minimal environmental disturbance and can also help to keep trails open for longer between maintenance periods.

Keep wildlife wild

Observe wildlife from a distance to prevent it fleeing – in hot or cold weather, disturbance can affect an animal's ability to withstand the environment. Do not feed wildlife you encounter, which can be harmful for the animals, and do not touch: this can be stressful for wildlife and dangerous for you if animals harbour rabies or other diseases.

Be fire smart

Research and heed fire rules in your destination; these are typically listed on national park websites. If you must smoke, carry a butt bin, and if you use a campfire, ensure it's completely extinguished before you move on. When hiking in bushfire (wildfire) season, keep a close eye on weather reports and fire monitoring websites and apps.

Keep your kit natural

If you're going to be cooking or washing in the wilderness, ensure that the soap, detergent and toiletries you use are gentle on the environment.

Give back

Help protect the wilderness areas you love by donating to or volunteering with an organisation dedicated to the cause. For example, the Center for Outdoor Ethics (www.lnt.org) maintains a volunteer registry, while Scottish conservation charity Trees for Life (www.treesforlife.org) runs 'conservation week' programmes open to the public.

Tips for responsible diving and snorkelling

Clapping eyes on a coral reef for the first time can be a transformative experience. But with a million new scuba divers certified by PADI alone each year, marine tourists are putting more pressure on aquatic ecosystems than ever. Take these tips on board to ensure your impact is minimal.

Watch your fins

One errant fin kick (or knock from unsecured diving equipment) that breaks a coral might not seem like a biggie, but if every snorkeller and diver who visited that site had the same attitude, the damage would soon add up. And while it goes without saying that you should never stand on the reef, a sandy-looking sea bed can be just as fragile. Unless your dive guide confirms it won't harm organisms, stay off the ocean floor.

Control your buoyancy

Buoyancy is key to ensuring you don't need to touch anything to stabilise yourself underwater. Copy the positioning of your dive guide and ask for feedback on how you can improve. Not only will you be protecting the reef, but you'll also conserve your air.

Don't feed the fish

It may seem innocent to feed marine life, but fish can become reliant on the practice, throwing their whole ecosystem out of whack. Damselfish, for example, graze on the algae that competes with coral for space and light. Attracting them with free food can see a reef shift to an algae-dominated state, which doesn't make for pleasant sightseeing.

ECO-HACK

Many dive centres have a no-gloves policy to help prevent divers touching the reef. If you're worried about stings and cuts from organisms on mooring lines, take one glove to hold on to the line while you descend and keep it in your pocket until you ascend.

© CHRIS CHEN / LONELY PLANET

Take only pictures

Shells provide homes for ocean critters, help to replenish sand and maintain the ocean's chemical balance. Dead coral is also recycled by the reef, so think twice about removing it from the beach, and avoid purchasing ocean products such as shell jewellery.

Leave only bubbles

Cigarette butts, plastic bottles, sweet wrappers – these are all items easily blown off a dive boat, so avoid bringing them on board. Even better, pick up any rubbish you spot in the water. Stuff it into the pocket of your buoyancy control device (BCD) or bring a mesh bag along to store rubbish in.

Take photos with care

Multiple academic studies have found that divers with cameras make the most contact with the reef, often causing coral to break as they steady themselves for a shot. If you're not a highly experienced diver, consider leaving your camera on the boat.

Give marine life space

Touching or crowding marine life can have various negative consequences, from exposing it to infection or, in the case of turtles, causing them to drown. The National Oceanic Atmospheric Administration (NOAA) in the US advises people to keep a distance of at least 3m (10ft) from turtles and 15m (50ft) from seals. Breaking the rules can incur fines in some destinations.

Choose responsible operators

Responsible snorkelling and diving operators keep groups small, provide comprehensive pre-immersion briefings and are strict on clients who demonstrate bad behaviour. The Green Fins website (www. greenfins.net) helps locate operators actively working to improve practices above and below the water.

Be respectful of your dive group

Listen carefully to your dive guide's briefing and stay with your buddy and in sight of the rest of the group. Nothing ruins a dive like a diver so absorbed in their own experience that they hold up the rest of the group.

Give back

Find or create your own ocean conservation action, report ocean debris and more via global ocean protection non-profit Project Aware (www. projectaware.org). Many dive centres also run beach or ocean clean-ups and other conservation initiatives which visitors can get involved in.

Tips for responsible safaris

© SERRNOVIK / GETTY IMAGES

Tracking animals in the wildest corners of the planet is an ultimate travel thrill. Ironically, these indulgent holidays typically take place in some of the world's poorest settings, and travellers have an important role to play in encouraging the safari industry to raise its standards.

Choose a responsible operator

Tours in delicate ecosystems call for operators with a strong commitment to tread lightly. Ensure your operator has a comprehensive responsible tourism policy and, where possible, stay in community-run lodges, ideally on community-owned land (known as conservancies).

Stay in your vehicle

Big game may appear docile from the safety of your vehicle, but if you get out, the situation can change in an instant, putting you, your travel companions and wildlife at risk – animals that attack humans are often euthanised. Only ever leave the vehicle if your guide advises it's safe, and if you're self-driving, abide by park rules.

Avoid peak periods

Timing your trip to coincide with events like Africa's wildebeest migration might see you share the

Serengeti with more tourists than wildlife and there's no excitement in safari park traffic jams. Visiting in the shoulder or low season is not only cheaper but helps to ensure year-round employment for local people.

Look beyond the popular parks

For every well-known game reserve there's a lesser-known option that offers an incredible – sometimes an even more incredible – wildlife-watching opportunity. In Africa, Malawi has only recently opened up for wildlife tourism, while in Nepal, Bardia National Park has more tigers than Chitwan, but less crowds.

Never handle wildlife

Resist opportunities to cuddle or 'walk with' big cats at so-called sanctuaries you may encounter on a safari holiday in Africa. This popular tourism experience has been condemned by conservationists who argue the industry is not only cruel (with lions typically sold on to canned hunting farms) but also has no conservation value.

Be a responsible photographer

Avoid disturbing wildlife by turning off the flash and focus beep on your camera and resisting the urge to make noises or hand gestures to attract animals. When photographing smaller game on walking safaris, use a long lens rather than crowding the creatures.

Opt for a walking safari

Carbon-neutral walking safaris are healthier for the planet and they offer an opportunity to connect with the environment and local guides on a deeper level than on vehicle-based safaris – a clear win-win. Maybe you'll learn how to identify animal tracks, discover bush foods, or enjoy the primal thrill of observing big game at eye level.

ECO-HACK

Keep your safari outfit neutral: brightly coloured clothing can scare off wildlife. In Africa, be mindful that blue and black clothing can attract tsetse flies, which have a nasty bite.

Think before you share

Sadly, poachers are known to use social media to locate targets. Avoid assisting them by not using geotags nor providing specific information about the location of wildlife in pictures you share on social media. Even better, wait a few days before posting pictures online.

Respect your guide

Egging on your guide to position you closer to wildlife, drive dangerously or behave in other unethical ways may make them feel pressured to abide by your wishes in order to be tipped. Don't put them in that position and remember to tip fairly.

Give back

Poaching remains the biggest threat to African wildlife. Help stamp it out by donating to organisations dedicated to fighting it such as the World Wildlife Fund (www.wwf.org), International Anti-Poaching Foundation (www.iapf.org), Wildlife Conservation Society (www.wcs.org) and Wild Foundation (www.wild.org).

INSPIRATION

Top five overland bus journeys

Improved domestic flight networks and the rise of cushy tourist transfer services have lured many a traveller away from bone-rattling local buses. But in many places, taking the bus is an essential experience. Here are five bus journeys you won't want to miss.

San Pedro de Atacama to Salta, South America
Distance: 600km (373 miles)
Estimated duration: 10 hours
South America's extensive, affordable bus system is ideal for exploring the vast continent. A leg to remember is the trip across the Andes from San Pedro de Atacama in northern Chile to Salta in Argentina. Passing snow-white salt flats, lunar-like ridges and topaz lakes sparkling against a backdrop of mountain peaks, before descending through the coloured hills of Salta province, you'll want a window seat.

Open Bus, Vietnam
Distance: 1730km (1075 miles)
Estimated duration: at least a week
Rumbling along the coastal highway between Hanoi in the north and Ho Chi Minh City in the south, Vietnam's ultra-convenient hop-on, hop-off bus ticket system allows you to pause at popular destinations en route over the course of a month. Travel is only permitted in one direction, but you can stay in each location for as long as you like – but reserve onward journeys a day in advance.

Marrakesh to Er Rachidia, Morocco
Distance: 559km (347 miles)
Estimated duration: 11 hours
This achingly scenic voyage begins in Marrakesh before chugging up through the High Atlas via the tortuous Tizi n'Tichka pass (2260m/7415ft). It then meanders through an arid landscape of mud-brick kasbahs and palm groves to Ouarzazate, nicknamed 'Ouallywood' for its film studio, before ending in Er Rachidia, a former French garrison town on the fringe of the Sahara, where desert adventures await.

Kathmandu to Pokhara, Nepal
Distance: 200km (124 miles)
Estimated duration: 8 hours
Sick bags are handed out at the beginning of this legendary hippie-trail journey that rattles from the Nepalese capital to the lakeside city of Pokhara, the gateway to the Annapurna region, tracing the bends of aqua-blue glacial rivers gurgling through the valleys below. At times you may think you can walk faster, but it's all part of the experience.

Great Ocean Road, Australia
Distance: 112km (70 miles)
Estimated duration: 2½ hours
Tracing the dramatic coastline of southwest Victoria, Australia's best-known scenic drive isn't only for private, petrol-guzzling vehicles. V/Line buses (www.vline.com.au) travel the route from Warrnambool to Melbourne via Apollo Bay and Geelong, stopping at the main sights of the Shipwreck Coast including the Bay of Islands, London Bridge, Loch Ard Gorge and the Twelve Apostles. Though service isn't daily, the bus takes the same gorgeous curves as the most dashing roadster.

Top five green rail journeys

It's no secret train travel is more energy efficient – and often far more enjoyable – than flying and driving, but some rail companies are greener than others. Here are five scenic rail journeys you can feel particularly good about.

Darjeeling Himalayan Express, India

Riding India's railways is a quintessential travel experience, now greener than ever following the banning of single-use plastics by Indian Railways in 2019. Bio-toilets are also currently being installed in its entire fleet. Snaking through emerald tea plantations from New Jalpaiguri to the hill station of Darjeeling, the Darjeeling Himalayan Railway is one of the company's prettiest journeys. www.indianrail.gov.in

Tōkaidō Shinkansen line, Japan

Japan's bullet-train network is powered by vastly efficient nuclear energy. With incredible views of Mt Fuji, the line that passes between Tokyo and Kyoto is arguably the most scenic route. It's also the first equipped with Central Japan Railways' new 'supreme' bullet trains, kinder to both the environment and passengers. https://global.jr-central.co.jp

Byron Bay Solar Train, Australia

The journey only takes 10 minutes, but the 3km (1.9-mile) trip from central Byron Bay to the town's thriving Arts & Industry Estate comes with bragging rights for riding the world's first fully solar-powered train. Passing through a coastal wetland, the journey in the restored 1940s 'red rattler' is suitably atmospheric. www.byronbaytrain.com.au

Eurail's Rhine Valley route, Germany

Connecting 31 European countries, the Eurail network reduces its impact by using recycled materials for travel packs and passes. One of its most charming routes hugs the bank of the River Rhine for some 97km (60 miles) as it wends along the valley from Koblenz to Mainz past half-timbered houses, vineyard-covered hills and winsome fairy-tale castles. www.eurail.com

Cape Town to Pretoria with Rovos Rail, South Africa

The luxury South African rail company's ecofriendly improvements range from stocking toilets with sugar-cane-derived Güdsheet loo roll (which provides TP to underprivileged schools) to sourcing produce for its on-board restaurant from sustainable local businesses. Rovos also supports many charitable initiatives, making the deluxe overland journey from Cape Town to Pretoria that much sweeter. www.rovos.com

ECO-HACK

Interested to know how the energy consumption of your rail journey compares with other forms of transport? Enter your journey details on the EcoPassenger website and see for yourself. www.ecopassenger.org

Top 10 electrifying road trips

The infrastructure for electric vehicles (EVs) has improved enormously around the world in recent years. As more destinations – and rental companies – make the electric leap, it's easier than ever to take an energy-efficient road trip. Here are ten to try.

National Tourist Route Hardangervidda, Norway

Designated for their breathtaking scenery, Norway's 18 tourist routes are well geared up for EVs, which, like the rest of the country, run almost entirely on renewable hydropower. If you only have time to tackle one route, journey from Bergen to take in the waterfalls and mountains in Hardangervidda National Park.

Garden Route, South Africa

It's now technically possible to drive all the way across South Africa without using a single drop of fuel, but with its coastal views, wineries, surf spots, wildlife reserves and myriad opportunities for adventure, the eight-hour holiday route from Cape Town to Port Elizabeth is the most rewarding section of the cross-country journey. It also has the lion's share of EV charging points.

Route 66, USA

Famous for attracting gas-guzzling Chevrolets and Cadillacs, the iconic 3243km (2015-mile) route from Chicago to Los Angeles has greened up big time, now with more than 130 EV charging points on the journey.

Barbados

Self-driving is easily the best way to explore this Caribbean island nation. Handily, Barbados is the world's third-highest user of EV technology. Leave no beach untouched while making the most of the

ECO-HACK

With a database of more than 290,000 EV charging points across the globe, the PlugShare website's free app is the ultimate digital sidekick for EV road-tripping. www.plugshare.com

island-wide charging system, with no more than 5km (3 miles) between each charging point.

Vancouver to Calgary, Canada

In 2019 Petro-Canada committed to adding 50 fast-charging EV stations across the Trans-Canada Highway, including in the sparsely served stretches of northern Ontario and the Prairies. Weaving through the Rocky Mountains, the most beautiful stretch of the highway from Vancouver to Calgary (973km/605 miles) is currently the best serviced by EV charging points.

Romantic Road, Germany

Germany may have fallen short of its ambitious plan to have one million electric cars on its roads by 2020, but it's still one of Europe's best equipped nations for EVs. Passing through Bavaria's most picturesque medieval villages, the 350km (217-mile) Romantic Road is a good place to start. www.romanticroadgermany.com

Golden Route, Japan

Japan is reported to have more EV charging stations than petrol stations, making EV road-tripping a

cinch. Take this busy route past Mt Fuji from Tokyo to Kyoto without spewing any fumes.

North Coast 500, Scotland

This 830km (516-mile) loop showcasing some of Scotland's finest coastal scenery now has more than 40 EV charging stations. Better yet, in 2018 Inverness-based all-electric car rental company Ecosse EV became one of the North Coast 500's official partners. www.northcoast500.com

Queensland's Electric Super Highway, Australia

The world's longest electric superhighway in a single state, this government initiative allows you to take a zero-emissions trip from Coolangatta to Cairns without a hint of range anxiety. To access the 14 'fast chargers' spread more or less evenly along the 1786km (1110-mile) coastal route, you'll need to register for a Chargefox (www.chargefox.com) account.

Ring Road, Iceland

The 2018 installation of an EV charging point in Mývatn officially opened the 1332km (828-mile) road encircling Iceland to EV drivers. To fully enjoy the incredible scenery – from geysers to glaciers, waterfalls to lava fields – allow at least a week to complete the journey.

Top five countries for budget green travel

Sustainable tourism in developing economies generally begins at the grassroots level. While it might need a little effort to seek out, the reward will be opportunities to experience local culture in an authentic setting while supporting your hosts directly.

Nepal

Nepal's rebuilding works following the devastating 2015 earthquakes are ongoing, so every tourist dollar counts. Recruiting guides and porters under fair conditions (see the International Porter Protection Group guidelines; www.ippg.net) is affordable and helps to support local communities. Reduce pressure on popular trails by opting for less-tramped hikes such as the Tamang Heritage Trail (see p92).

Estonia

Budget-friendly Estonia is surprisingly eco-conscious. Lahemaa, near Tallinn, became the Soviet Union's first national park in 1971, and in 2008 Estonia invented the concept of World Cleanup Day. Over 50% of Estonia is covered by forest, and green spaces offer serene ecotourism experiences, from cycling in virgin forests and paddling canoes across pristine lakes to Lahemaa National Park's Projekt Kodu, off-grid glamping with a unique outdoor spa (www.projekt-kodu.ee).

Laos

Sandwiched between Thailand and Vietnam, Laos' low population density – and relatively low visitor numbers – makes for a relaxed budget Southeast Asian adventure. In the north, ancient Luang Prabang city has a realm of social enterprises offering affordable tourism experiences designed to lift up the community, from a natural silk-dying workshop at women's weaving cooperative Ock Pop Tok (www.ockpoptok.com) to a delicious Laotian meal at Khaiphaen (www.tree-alliance.org), a Friends International–sponsored restaurant that trains underprivileged youths.

Nicaragua

In one of the Americas' cheapest travel destinations, a collective of farming communities have established tourism cooperatives offering unique experiences that promote sustainable socio-economic growth. Learn about organic farming and visit ancient petroglyphs at Finca Magdalena (www.fincamagdalena.com) near Granada, hike to Datanlí Nature Reserve waterfalls at Ecoalbergue La Fundadora (www.fundadora.org), and learn about sustainable coffee production from the folks who grow it at a UCA San Ramon Agro Ecotourism (www.tourism.ucasanramon.com) homestay.

North Macedonia

One of Europe's least-visited countries, North Macedonia has much on offer for travellers seeking a budget, low-impact escape. The recently opened High Scardus Trail (www.highscardustrail.com) is a 495km (308-mile) hiking route tracing the mountainous borders with Kosovo and Albania. Visit outside of the June to August high season to get the best from the country's natural areas, slow-food culture and capital Skopje's Ottoman-era bazaars.

Top five sustainable family trips

Travelling with kids provides boundless opportunities to teach younger generations about the fragility of ecosystems and the significance of heritage, both critical in learning how to live in harmony with the Earth.

Fiji

Several hotels, such as Jean-Michel Cousteau Resort and Fiji's two Outrigger resorts, invite guests to get involved in marine conservation projects like coral planting, offering kids a valuable lesson in the importance of reef systems. With older children, consider heading off the beaten track to lodge in a village homestay; or a multi-day hike between several villages with Tanaloa Treks (https://tanaloa-treks-fiji.com), where your tourist dollars directly support remote communities.

Ecuador

With unique free-roaming wildlife and a strict no-touch policy, there's no better place than the Galápagos Islands to teach kids about responsible wildlife tourism. Elsewhere, Ecuador's family-friendly eco-resorts include Mashpi Lodge (www.mashpilodge.com), which runs a Young Mashpi Rangers programme and has a discovery centre, while the socially responsible Tren Ecuador (www.trenecuador.com) tourist train supports local communities along its route through the country's 'Avenue of Volcanoes'.

New Zealand

With reams of scenic campsites, New Zealand was made for family campervan holidays – which got a lot greener in 2019, when rental company Britz (www.britz.com) launched its fully electric eVolve camper van in both islands. From the geothermal parks in Rotorua to the penguins of the Otago Peninsula, the nation's natural wonders alone will wow children of all ages, while bigger kids will love ecofriendly adventures from top-notch e-biking to scaling the world's highest waterfall via ferrata in Wanaka (www.wildwire.co.nz).

Wales

Despite its small size, Wales packs a big punch in terms of sustainable activities for kids. Find Pembrokeshire's green campsites via www.greenercamping.org, or have fun learning about sustainable living at Powys' Centre for Alternative Technology. Factor in a spin on the world's only people-powered roller coaster at the Snowdonia's Greenwood Forest Park (www.greenwoodfamilypark.com), and tuck into sustainably caught fish and chips at Penaluna's in the Brecon Beacons (www.penalunas.co.uk), best in Wales in the 2018 National Fish and Chip Awards.

Botswana

Peaceful Botswana is renowned for its wildlife conservation, with more than a quarter of the land set aside to conserve the country's natural heritage. Children under 12 are now welcomed with open arms at many safari lodges, where family programmes include wildlife tracking and making bows and arrows, while responsible travel operator Jumbari Family Safaris (www.jumbari.com) offers several

Top 10 sustainable cruises

Despite some efforts to clean up their act, these floating cities put intense pressure on the environment and on the ports they visit. Feel better about cruising by choosing smaller, expedition-style ships run by environmentally aware companies.

Melanesia

From the remote coastlines of Australia's Kimberley to the lesser-visited waterways of Papua New Guinea, Australian small-ship cruising company Coral Expeditions specialises in voyages in remote tropical waters. An EcoTourism Australia–certified 'Green Travel Leader', Coral also backs sustainability initiatives ranging from a crown-of-thorns starfish control programme to financially supporting several turtle sanctuaries. www.coralexpeditions.com

Norwegian Arctic

Sailing is of course the most sustainable form of cruising. On board Narwhal Expeditions' 15m yacht, you'll admire magical Arctic seascapes as well as help to gather data, enabling scientists to learn more about these fragile marine environments and how to protect them. Each year, the company runs a Clean Up The Arctic Expedition which sees volunteers conduct litter surveys, remove debris from beaches and participate in marine mammal population studies along the coastline of Svalbard. www.narwhalexpeditions.com

Pacific Northwest

Cruise hidden waterways in the Pacific Northwest (and beyond) that the big ships can't access with North American small-ship operator UnCruise Adventures, which has a particularly comprehensive responsible travel policy. On top of supporting local communities by purchasing local produce, using local guides and donating to local organisations, UnCruise's waste-reducing strategy extends to supplying reusable drink bottles and refillable bathroom amenities. www.uncruise.com

French Polynesia

Drop in on unspoilt villages in the cinematically beautiful Marquesas Islands, one of the most remote island groups in the world, on the Aranui 5 as the hybrid freighter-passenger ship makes its 13-day supply run. Offering a rare taste of local life, shore excursions include everything from visiting archaeological sites to taking in a local church service. www.aranui.com

© DAVID MERRON / GETTY IMAGES

Antarctica

The inventor of modern expedition cruising, Lindblad has eliminated single-use plastics across its fleet, buys sustainable seafood, makes crew uniforms from recycled plastic and is building new ships that reduce emissions. The company has helped to raise more than US$17 million in donations for conservation projects and, in 2019, also became the world's first cruise line to become carbon-neutral, making it a worthy option for exploring particularly fragile aquatic destinations like Antarctica. www.expeditions.com

Galápagos Islands

All vessels operating in Ecuador's Galápagos Islands must comply with stringent standards, but some are more ecofriendly than others. Enter Grand Queen Beatriz. Billed as the most sustainable cruise expedition in the region, carbon-neutral tour company Peregrine's first custom-made ship, which carries 16 passengers, was designed by a local boatbuilder and is equipped with the latest fuel-efficient technology, with some power generated by solar. Common single-use plastics are also banned on board. www.peregrineadventures.com

Andean Coast

In 2019 Norwegian cruise line Hurtigruten, which calls itself 'the world's greenest cruise line', launched the world's first hybrid-powered expedition ship. Named after the first man to cross Antarctica and reach the South Pole, the MS Roald Amundsen was designed to navigate polar waters with ease, but the ship's itineraries along the Andean Coast of South America present the perfect opportunity to explore lesser trafficked routes. www.hurtigruten.com

The Nile

Visit key attractions between Luxor and Aswan on a traditional Egyptian sailing boat known as a dahabiya. Not only are dahabiyas incredibly ecofriendly (a tug-boat assists only if there is no wind), but most companies are also locally owned. Accommodating a maximum of 18 guests at a time, Dahabiya Nile Sailing offers one of the most affordable yet comprehensive itineraries around. www.dahabiyanilesailing.com

The Danube

The only river cruise company operating on European waterways to be awarded the 'Green Certificate' seal of approval by Green Globe for its sustainability practices, family-run Amadeus was also Europe's first river cruise operator to introduce voluntary carbon offsetting, with the company contributing an extra 25% to each donation. Revel in the comfort of its newest vessel, Amadeus Star, which currently cruises five Danube routes. www.amadeus-rivercruises.com

The Mekong

It has only been in business for just over a decade, but boutique luxury river and yacht cruise line Aqua Expeditions has already established itself as a sustainable cruising leader. Designed and built in Vietnam with sustainable local materials, the luxurious Aqua Mekong is equipped with the latest ecofriendly technology, including low-emission engines and low-impact launch boats. It also uses ecofriendly cleaning products and has phased out single-use plastics. www.aquaexpeditions.com

Top 10 ecofriendly city breaks

Cities committed to lowering their carbon footprint make it easier for travellers to minimise their own. Here are ten cities making ecofriendly visits a walk in the park.

Vancouver, Canada

Canada's outdoor-adventure capital came impressively close to realising the lofty objectives of its Greenest City 2020 Action Plan outlined back in 2011. For visitors, vast improvements to the city's public transport networks – including the launch of the Mobi bike-share scheme – have made it easier than ever to get around without a car. Plastic straws, foam cups and takeaway containers were also banned in 2020.

★ **Don't leave without:** Cycling amid 400 hectares of natural West Coast rainforest in the city's green lung, Stanley Park.

★ **Sustainable stay:** Centrally located Skwachàys Lodge takes sustainability into the social environment, with a portion of profits from the 18-room hotel helping to subsidise housing units for indigenous artists in the same restored Victorian building. www.skwachays.com

Copenhagen, Denmark

Sustainability has long been top priority in Denmark, with Copenhagen widely considered to be the world's greenest city. Life runs on two wheels here – with more than five bikes for every car in the capital, it's easy to get around via the city's Bycyklen bike-share scheme, or perhaps explore its waterways by electric GoBoat. Most restaurants use organic local produce, and the harbour is so clean you can swim in it!

★ **Don't leave without:** Skiing down CopenHill, an artificial urban ski slope built atop a waste-to-power plant. The complex also has an 85m-high (280ft) climbing wall. www.copenhill.dk

★ **Sustainable stay:** Copenhagen hotel group Brøchner was the first company in Denmark to open a chemical-free hotel. Its newest pad, Hotel Ottilia, opened in 2019 in the old Carlsberg Brewery and boasts the same credentials – plus a free daily wine hour. www.brochner-hotels.com/hotel-ottilia

Cape Town, South Africa

Cape Town proved its sustainability chops in its response to the 2018 'Day Zero' water crisis, which revolutionised the city's relationship with water. The threat has since passed yet consumption has stayed low, with visitors encouraged to follow the locals' leads by having shorter showers, only flushing when necessary and embracing hand sanitiser.

★ **Don't leave without:** Hiking (or taking the carbon-neutral cable car) to the top of Table Mountain for staggering city and water views.
★ **Sustainable stay:** Certified by Fair Trade Tourism, a non-profit that recognises best practice in Africa, The Backpack hostel encourages guests to give back to the community through initiatives such as knitting a square for blankets distributed to orphanages. A host of other green measures include on-site worm farms taking care of composting vegetable waste. www.backpackers.co.za

Singapore

The city state's S$300 fines for littering, strict green building laws and novel attempts to preserve its green spaces (or in the case of the Jewel Changi Airport complex, create new ones) are all testaments to Singapore's commitment to becoming one of the world's greenest cities. While the government has been reluctant to impose single-use plastic bans, the issue is a growing concern among locals.

★ **Don't leave without:** Walking through the treetops on the elevated walkways that form part of the 10km (6-mile) Southern Ridges trail linking five parks and reserves.
★ **Sustainable stay:** Designed to seamlessly blend technology with the environment, the luxe Parkroyal on Pickering hotel's waterfalls, self-sustaining landscaped roof terraces and vertical gardens help to keep the building blissfully cool. www.panpacific.com

Edinburgh, UK

The Scottish city regularly tops greenest UK city lists and for good reason. An impressive 49% of Edinburgh is green space, electric vehicle charging points are aplenty, and many businesses have glowing eco-credentials. Leading the way is the Edinburgh Fringe; on top of taking steps to limit the impact of the annual comedy festival, it has developed a comprehensive guide to help the industry run greener shows.

★ **Don't leave without:** Making the 251m (822ft) climb to Arthur's Seat for superb views of the city skyline, perhaps with a healthy, plastic-free picnic lunch from Hula Juice Bar. www.hulajuicebar.co.uk
★ **Sustainable stay:** Start the day with an organic, locally sourced breakfast at eco-conscious family-run McCraes Bed & Breakfast, set in a Victorian town house in Edinburgh's New Town. www.mccraes.co.uk

Bogotá, Colombia

Colombia's capital hasn't just been busy cleaning up its image, but also greening it. The introduction of mass rapid-transit buses and the closing of main streets to vehicle traffic on Sundays have played a major role in curbing air pollution, and green building is taking off. Restaurants, too, are getting in on the act, with sustainable-minded and vegan-friendly cafes like Canasto Picnic Bistró (www.facebook.com/canastopicnicbistro) currently all the rage.

★ **Don't leave without:** Exploring the city's parks, plazas and historical monuments while learning about its turbulent history on two wheels with Bogotá Bike Tours. www.bogotabiketours.com

★ **Sustainable stay:** In the leafy Usaquén neighbourhood, Biohotel Organic Suites combines luxury with the utmost respect for the environment. There's an extensive solar set-up, organic linens, renewable wood furnishings, and carpets made from fully recycled materials. Even the gym equipment generates power while in use. www.biohotelcolombia.com

San Francisco, USA

The first US city to ban plastic bags, San Francisco is also in the vanguard when it comes to waste disposal, water management, ecofriendly buildings and green transportation – its buses run on biodiesel, and more than 60% of taxis run on alternative fuel. Plastic straws were banned citywide in 2019, as were plastic water bottles at San Francisco Airport. Many eateries have also embraced compostable crockery, taking the stress out of takeaway dining.

★ **Don't leave without:** Shopping for vintage threads on Valencia St in the Mission district and Haight St in the Haight-Ashbury district.

★ **Sustainable stay:** On Fisherman's Wharf, the nautical-themed Argonaut Hotel's respectable eco-initiatives extend to its in-house restaurant, Blue Mermaid, which is committed to serving

sustainable seafood and recycles kitchen grease into biofuel. www.argonauthotel.com

Wellington, New Zealand

Having enshrined the country's commitment to the Paris Agreement in law in late 2019, New Zealand is well on the way to achieving zero net carbon dioxide emissions by 2050. With the lowest emissions per capita of any Australasian city, Wellington is at the forefront of the movement. Packed with world-class cultural institutions, eco-conscious cafes (many of which operate 'mug libraries'), the compact capital is best explored on foot.

★ **Don't leave without:** Touring Zealandia, the world's first fully fenced urban sanctuary designed to restore a Wellington valley's forest floor and freshwater ecosystems to their pre-human state. www.visitzealandia.com

★ **Sustainable stay:** The luxurious, centrally located Bolton Hotel is committed to buying locally and minimising energy and waste, with recycling stations throughout the hotel inviting guests to follow suit. www.boltonhotel.co.nz

Tel Aviv, Israel

It's home to one of the world's largest waste dump regeneration projects (Ariel Sharon Park) and its mostly flat streets are ideal for exploring via the city's Tel-O-Fun bike-share scheme, but when it comes to sustainability Tel Aviv particularly excels in the food space. Dubbed the vegan capital of the world, most of the city's restaurants offer plenty of plant-based options using produce grown in an increasing network of rooftop gardens.

★ Don't leave without: Learning just how good vegan cuisine can taste at the city's 400-odd vegan and vegan-friendly restaurants, such as Bana. www.banatlv.com

★ Sustainable stay: On top of its energy-saving and responsible waste disposal initiatives and strong stance against single-use plastic, slick boutique hotel The Vera is also furnished exclusively by home-grown artisans, right down to the organic bathroom amenities. www.theverahotel.com

Oslo, Norway

The European Green Capital of 2019 is quite literally electric. Not only is it the world's electric car capital, but in 2019 it also rolled out an electric scooter-share scheme, and its ferries are being progressively electrified. Even the hottest new attraction in town – the 13-floor Munch Museum, opened in 2020 – was built to strict ecofriendly standards.

★ Don't leave without: Embracing Oslo's urban sauna culture at one of Oslo Fjord Sauna's four floating saunas. Docked in Bjørvika, the Måken sauna was made entirely out of driftwood and recycled materials. www.oslofjordsauna.com

★ Sustainable stay: Part of the Vulcan sustainable urban development in the hip Grünerløkka neighbourhood, PS:Hotel focuses on employing people who've struggled for various reasons to gain a foothold in the labour market. www.pshotell.no

Top 10 low-impact multi-day hikes

The ultimate form of slow travel, hiking holidays offer an incredible opportunity to exercise while connecting with nature and local communities. Lace your boots for these memorable and sustainable hiking adventures.

Tamang Heritage Trail, Nepal
Duration: 6 days
This seldom-tramped loop trail on the western edge of Langtang National Park, north of Kathmandu, might be riddled with mountain views, but unlike more popular Himalayan treks it passes through remote culturally Tibetan Tamang villages where daily life has changed little over the centuries. By staying off the tourist trail in basic family-owned teahouses built for traders rather than tourists, you're providing an income for Tamang communities which were badly affected by Nepal's 2015 earthquakes.

Via Francigena, Italy
Duration: 16 days
For many, the highlight of this ancient 2000km (1243-mile) pilgrimage route linking Canterbury in England to Rome is the 354km (219-mile) Tuscan section, which comprises 16 legs of the journey. As you hike through rolling vineyards and sleepy medieval villages where locals still leave their doors unlocked, you'll feel a world away from the tourist-choked piazzas of Florence and Siena. www.viefrancigene.org

Cirque de Mafate, Réunion
Duration: 3–5 days
The only way into the Cirque de Mafate, one of three volcanic amphitheatres on this French-administered Indian Ocean island, is on foot. Handy, then, that the lush caldera's handful of tiny villages, waterfalls, deep gorges and jungly peaks are linked by an achingly scenic and refreshingly uncrowded loop trail. Many locals make their living running gîtes (guesthouses), offering an authentic mountain homestay experience complete with the best Creole curries you'll taste on the island.

Transcaucasian Trail, Armenia and Georgia
Duration: 5–7 days per leg
When completed, this 3000km (1864-mile) trail weaving through the Greater and Lesser Caucasus Mountains is set to be one of the most epic long-distance hikes on the planet. Several sections are already open (including the 125km/78-mile Vayots Dzor leg in Armenia, which opened in 2019) and two-week trail-building programmes are available to travellers keen to play an active role in the trail's completion. www.transcaucasiantrail.org

Salkantay Trail, Peru
Duration: 4–5 days
Help to reduce pressure on the iconic Inca Trail by opting for this higher-altitude route to Machu Picchu, which delivers superb views of the trail's namesake, the highest peak in Peru's Vilcabamba mountain range, en route. Reaching a maximum altitude of 4600m (15,090ft), the challenging Salkantay Trail ends at the town of Aguas Calientes, at the base of the famous Inca ruin.

Wukalina Walk, Australia

Duration: 4 days

Launched in 2018, Tasmania's first Palawa (Tasmanian Aboriginal) owned and run guided hiking experience introduces you to the 10,000-odd years of Aboriginal history and culture connected to the stunning larapuna (Bay of Fires) and wukalina (Mt William) areas in the state's northeast, over the course of a manageable 34km (21-mile) trail. www.wukalinawalk.com.au

Mt Kenya, Kenya

Duration: 2–4 days

Atop Kenya's highest peak you can survey Africa from on high while dodging the big crowds of Mt Kilimanjaro. Mt Kenya actually has three peaks, with most hikers opting for Point Lenana (4985m/16355ft), the least technical. While guides aren't mandatory, hiring one makes a valuable contribution to the local economy, which has been struggling to contend with the effects of the mountain's shrinking glaciers.

Historical Way, Portugal

Duration: 10 days

Part of the Rota Vicentina network of hiking trails that criss-crosses Portugal's countryside, the 263km (163-mile) Historical Way includes 13 sections linking rural villages well off the tourist trail. Strongly committed to responsible travel, the private company that maintains the trails works closely with local people to create unique guest experiences that help to protect this pristine region. www.rotavicentina.com

Jordan Trail, Jordan

Duration: 40 days

Opened in 2017, this 650km (404-mile) trail from Jordan's tip to tail presents the ultimate alternative perspective on the country. Most hikers tackle one or more of the eight sections – the sixth leg, linking the otherworldly Dana Biosphere to the ancient city of Petra over four days, offers the added opportunity to spend your first night at Feynan Ecolodge (www.ecohotels.me), one of the world's top eco-lodges. www.jordantrail.org

Long Trail, USA

Duration: 19 days

Vermont consistently ranks as one of the greenest states in the US, which makes hiking the 169km (272-mile) wilderness trail that traverses its length all the sweeter. With more than 70 backcountry campsites and 103km (166 miles) of side trails to choose from, there are endless ways to tackle this classic yet often overlooked trail.

TOP TIP

What Guyana lacks in traditional handicraft shopping opportunities it makes up for in excellent local products, from peanut butter to coconut oil, hot sauces to curry spices. Stock up at the Guyana Shop in Georgetown (cnr Robb and Alexander Streets).

Practicalities

✈ Georgetown

🚌 It's possible to enter Guyana overland from Brazil at Lethem, which is handy for visiting Rupununi region lodges. From Georgetown, the journey to Paramaribo, Suriname's capital, takes roughly nine hours, including a ferry ride at the border.

💼 Light, long-sleeved clothing, a hat, and more sunscreen and insect repellent than you think you'll need are essentials for the interior. Binoculars will greatly enhance wildlife-watching.

📅 Kaieteur Falls is breathtaking year-round, but it's at its fullest immediately after the main rainy season (May to early August), making this an ideal time to visit. Access to the interior can be an issue during the wetter months.

$ $ $

Guyana

Guyana is home to the world's highest single-drop waterfall and 18% of the planet's tropical forests; better yet, its tourism industry is focused on developing sustainable experiences that safeguard indigenous Amerindian culture and promote conservation.

Sandwiched between Venezuela and Suriname, sleepy Guyana has been described as South America's best-kept secret. And it's easy to see why. With empty Atlantic beaches in the north, dramatic mountain ranges in the west, vast savannahs in the south and wild tracts of jungle bursting with wildlife in between, this former British colony is the ultimate playground for intrepid 21st-century explorers.

As many other countries scramble to manage the impacts of unsustainable tourism development, Guyana has been blessed with the rare opportunity to get tourism right before it takes off. Many of the lodges in its remote interior are community-owned and -run, which encourages locals to stay in their villages rather than leave to seek work in mining or logging.

© TANE-MAHUTA / GETTY IMAGES

Nailing sustainable travel in Guyana

★ Eco-lodges and ranch stays are remote. Avoid putting unnecessary pressure on lodge hosts by ensuring you have packed the right gear and medical supplies.

★ Guyana does not currently have any recycling facilities, so you may wish to leave some space in your pack to bring some recyclables home with you.

★ Politely decline offers to visit schools in remote communities. Amongst other issues, tourist visits disrupt classes.

★ Take the local bus to or from the interior rather than flying.

★ It's crucial to use ecofriendly toiletries on jungle expeditions.

★ Factor in a side trip to neighbouring Suriname, which is accessible by land.

97 SUSTAINABLE TRAVEL HANDBOOK

GREEN STAYS

★ Deep in Guyana's jungly heart, Rewa Eco-Lodge – one of the nation's more established community-run eco-lodges – provides an authentic setting for Rupununi River adventures with Amerindian guides. www.rewaecolodge.com

★ Birdwatch from the canopy walk or wander jungle trails in search of jaguar at the charming and efficiently run Atta Rainforest Lodge in the Iwokrama Forest, one of the world's last pristine rainforests. www.attarainforestlodge.com

★ In Guyana's northwest, Warapoka Lodge offers a community-based tourism experience beyond the Rupununi. It's a great base for harpy-eagle-spotting. Book via www.wilderness-explorers.com

GIVE BACK

★ Basic necessities such as clothes, children's toys, school supplies and over-the-counter medical supplies are always needed in remote communities. Consider the sustainability of things like toys before purchasing, and donate to a community elder or lodge manager rather than directly to children.

★ The Rupununi Learners Foundation based at Caiman House has funded the construction of classroom libraries and a public library in the village and aims to support other communities with similar resources. Bring some books to donate or contact the foundation to enquire if there are other supplies they may need. www.rupununilearners.org

© WARAPOKA LODGE

© WARAPOKA LODGE

Previous page, from left: Kaiteur Falls; jaguars roam free in Guyana's jungles.
Left: harpy eagle and tropical plantlife at Warapoka Lodge.
Opposite: aerial view over Caiman House Lodge.

INSPO AND INFO

📖 *Wild Coast: Travels on South America's Untamed Edge* by John Gimlette (2011)
📖 Lonely Planet's *South America guidebook*
🎬 *Jungle Fish* (2012)
🎙 *Guyana – bracing for the oil boom*, BBC World Service (2019)

HANDY APP

For useful info including bridge reports and ferry schedules, bus stop locations and more, download the Guyana's Home app.

Ultimate sustainable travel experiences

★ Spotting Guyana's incredible wildlife – from giant otters to black caiman, and perhaps even jaguars – on walking and river safaris hosted by eco-lodges in the interior.

★ Admiring the power of Kaieteur Falls, which is twice as high as Africa's Victoria Falls.

★ Sampling Guyanese cuisine at Backyard Cafe, a dining experience hosted by passionate Guyanese cook Delven Adam in his own backyard. www.facebook.com/backyardcafeonline

★ Spreading your tourism dollars beyond Guyana's big hitters by exploring the emerging tourism potential of southern Rupununi and beyond.

★ Learning about grassroots wildlife protection while staying at Karanambu Lodge (www.karanambutrustandlodge.org) and Caiman House (www.caimanhouse.com) in the Central Rupunini, conservation centres which are funded by tourist visits.

TOP TIP
Hobart's harbourside Salamanca Market, held on Saturdays, is a great spot to pick up local produce and locally made souvenirs.

Practicalities

✈️ Hobart; Launceston

⚓ Ferries run between Melbourne and Davenport, Tasmania, at least once daily (10hr).

💼 The Tasmanian wilderness can be unforgiving, with most multi-day trails requiring a high level of self-sufficiency. Essentials include proper hiking boots, wet-weather gear and a well-stocked first aid kit.

📅 Tasmania is a year-round destination, but many activity operators close during the chilly winter months (late May to late September). Hikers should be prepared for snow on higher-altitude trails during this period.

$ $ $

Tasmania

With nearly half of its territory protected by national parks and preserves, Tasmania really is Australia's greenest state. Framed by pristine beaches and laced with hiking and mountain-biking trails, it's the stuff outdoor adventures are made of.

Once mocked as a backwater, 'Tassie' is now one of Australia's fastest-growing tourism destinations. But while its increasing popularity has come with its challenges, the state is focused on ensuring the industry evolves sustainably. It's a joint effort in Tassie – the home of the world's first green political party – where local produce plays a starring role at restaurants, hotels are moving to ban single-use plastics en masse, and activity operators are committed to ensuring clients tread lightly, all of which help to safeguard one of the last truly wild places on Earth.

Nailing sustainable travel in Tasmania

★ Ensure you're well prepared for wilderness walks by watching the safety video on the Tasmania Parks & Wildlife Service website before you go. www.parks.tas.gov.au

★ Whatever you take into wilderness areas should be packed out, right down to apple cores and toilet paper.

★ Use ecofriendly toiletries when camping to help minimise your environmental impact.

★ Help limit the volume of goods flown in or shipped to the island by choosing places to eat that showcase local produce.

© URASA BURAPACHEEP / GETTY IMAGES

★ Avoid arriving by large cruise ship, which have been blamed for 'overwhelming' Hobart.

★ Follow the Australian Marine Conservation Society's advice to avoid eating farmed Atlantic 'Tasmanian' salmon due to environmental concerns.

GREEN STAYS

★ Australia's first 'storytelling hotel', MACq 01 encourages guests at the swish harbourside hotel to help make plastic a 'story of the past' by embracing Hobart's pure tap water. www.macq01.com.au

★ Watch wild quolls and Tasmanian devils feeding from the comfort of one of five Mountain Valley Wilderness Holidays–managed log cabins, nestled in a conservation reserve near Cradle Mountain. www.mountainvalley.com.au

★ The Three Capes Track (www.threecapestrack.com.au) has stylish, eco-sensitive, architect-designed hiking huts. Tasmania Walking Company (www.taswalkingco.com.au) also offers a guided option staying in luxurious eco-lodges tucked off the trail.

GIVE BACK

★ Adopt a penguin for as little as AU$20 through Wildcare Tasmania, a not-for-profit that relies on donations to fund state-wide conservation efforts, from caring for injured wildlife to developing community awareness. www.wildcaretas.org.au

★ Sign up for a volunteering stint with Conservation Volunteers Australia, which runs projects in Tasmania ranging from rehabilitating habitat for birds and wildlife to beach clean-ups. www.conservationvolunteers.com.au

★ Get behind Tasmania Conservation Trust's environmental campaigns by signing petitions and donating to the causes it supports. www.tasconservation.org.au

© ALASTAIR_BETT

© PORT ARTHUR HISTORIC SITE

Previous page, from left: Wineglass Bay is just one of Tasmania's many stunning coves; a wallaby hits the beach. **Left:** Port Arthur, on the ground and from above. **Opposite:** the waterside deck at MACq 01.

INSPO AND INFO

📖 *An Activist Life* by Christine Milne (2017)
📖 *The Black War: Fear, Sex and Resistance in Tasmania* by Nicholas Clements (2014)
📖 Lonely Planet's *Tasmania guidebook*
🎬 *Saving Martha* (2019)

HANDY APP

Tick off Tasmania Parks & Wildlife Service's 60 Great Short Walks via your smartphone. www.parks.tas.gov.au

Ultimate sustainable travel experiences

★ Exploring the state's 880-odd hiking trails, from the multi-day Overland and Three Capes tracks, to seaside day walks in Freycinet National Park and wildlife in Narawntapu National Park.

★ Learning about Palawa (Tasmanian Aboriginal) culture and history on the four-day, Aboriginal-owned and -guided Wukalina Walk.

★ Taking a spin in the world-class Maydena Mountain Bike Park, or along the Blue Derby Mountain Bike Trails network.

★ Sampling Tasmania's local produce: gourmet cheeses, freshly shucked oysters, cool-climate wines and award-winning small-batch whiskies.

★ Drifting along Tassie's sparkling waterways on a kayak. For excellent chances of spotting a platypus, sign up for Tassie Bound's Paddle with the Platypus tour. www.tassiebound.com.au

★ Visiting during the winter (low) season to take in the Museum of Old and New Art's Dark Mofo Festival (www.darkmofo.net.au) as well as the World Heritage-listed Port Arthur Historic Site. www.portarthur.org.au

TOP TIP

If you're visiting between March and October, don't miss the opportunity to eat your way around Slovenia at Ljubljana's excellent (and low-waste) Open Kitchen market held on Fridays. www. odprtakuhna.si

Practicalities

✈ Ljubljana

🚌 Buses connect Ljubljana to Zagreb, Croatia (2¼ hours); Venice, Italy (4 hours); Vienna, Austria (6 hours) and Budapest, Hungary (7½ hours). Trains fly the same routes, with similar journey times.

💼 Good-quality walking shoes and comfortable clothes you can move in are ideal for getting stuck into Slovenia's wealth of outdoor activities and adventures.

📅 Aim for the April to May and September to October shoulder seasons. It might be a little chilly for swimming, but it's perfect weather for hiking and hotels are cheaper. There's also decent, affordable skiing during the winter months.

$ $

Slovenia

The tiny Adriatic nation is only 30 years old, but Slovenia is already light years ahead of many other EU countries in terms of sustainability, with myriad protected areas, extensive low-emissions transport networks and an emphasis on natural local produce.

With more than 500 sq m (538 sq ft) of public green space per resident and a beautiful historic core closed to traffic, Ljubljana, a former European Green Capital, is one of the continent's most walkable cities. In the surrounding countryside, some of Europe's best ecotourism adventures await. Most travellers will visit picture-postcard Lake Bled, Slovenia's famous subterranean cave systems and perhaps sign up for a few outdoor activities in the Soča Valley, but beyond the popular attractions lie dozens of blissfully uncrowded medieval villages, family wineries, hiking trails, thermals spas and more.

Nailing sustainable travel in Slovenia

★ Brush up on all things Slovenia (including language) via the excellent free Slovene Learning Online programme developed by the University of Ljubljana. www.slonline.si

★ Don't forget your reusable carrier bag; plastic bags were banned in Slovenian supermarkets in 2019.

★ If you're planning to hire a car, go electric; Slovenia's plentiful charging stations are mapped on the Gremo na Elektriko website. www.gremonaelektriko.si

★ Pick up a jar of Slovenian honey; one in 20 people keep

© OPEN KITCHEN

bees in Slovenia, and local honey products are traceable.

★ Embrace tap water: Slovenia has some of the world's best drinking water.

★ Consider skipping the flight and travelling via bus or train from one of Slovenia's four neighbouring countries.

GREEN STAYS

★ Ljubljana's leading green hotel, B&B Hotel Ljubljana Park recycles nearly 100% of its waste and has its own beehives and electric car charging station. www.hotelpark.si

★ Near Lake Bled, the AMS Beagle is furnished by local artisans, cleaned with ecofriendly products and serves an excellent local-produce breakfast. www.amsbeagle.com

★ In the Karst region, charming Hotel St Daniel takes a holistic approach to eco-hospitality. Rooms are decorated with recycled materials and stocked with organic toiletries, and the excellent restaurant showcases organic local produce. www.stdaniel.si

GIVE BACK

★ Make time for a light and nutritious Slovenian meal at Ljubljana's Gostilna Dela, a social enterprise restaurant that acts as a vocational training centre for vulnerable and disabled young people. www.gostilnadela.si

★ For African, Asian and South American food, head to social enterprise restaurant Skuhna, also in the capital, which empowers migrants through culinary work while helping to promote cultural understanding and exchange. www.skuhna.si

★ Support German charity Euronatur, which campaigns against the hunting of brown bears in Slovenia and drives the establishment of bear conservation areas. www.euronatur.org

© OPEN KITCHEN

© HOTEL LJUBLJANA PARK

Previous page, from left: Lake Bled paddleboarding; Ljubljana's Open Kitchen market. **From far left:** Open Kitchen cooking; rooftop beekeeping at Hotel Ljubljana Park. **Opposite:** rest stop on the Bike Slovenia Green route.

INSPO AND INFO

📖 Lonely Planet's *guidebook to Slovenia*
🎞 *The Undamaged* (2018)
🎞 *City of Light* (2017)
🎙 *Land of Dreams*, ongoing

HANDY APP

Find the nearest bike-share station, check how many bikes are available and how many parking spaces are free with Ljubljana's Bicikelj bike-sharing app. http://en.bicikelj.si

Ultimate sustainable travel experiences

★ Drinking your way around Slovenia's excellent yet hugely underrated wineries, many of which produce natural wines. There are plenty of craft beers to try, too.

★ Tackling the new 'Bike Slovenia Green' cycling routes which have been rolled out in 12 Slovenia Green– certified locations; sign up with Ljubljana-based operator and trail designer Visit Good Place. www.visit-goodplace. com

★ Hiking in the Julian Alps; avoid the crowds on Mt Triglav, Slovenia's highest peak, by aiming for an ascent in June or July, when flowers are in bloom.

★ Hiking, rafting, kayaking, mountain biking and even skiing in the Soča Valley, home to one of the most beautiful rivers in Europe.

★ Visiting during the colder months, when you can enjoy the winter wonderland of Lake Bled largely to yourself, and go skiing in Kranjska Gora.

TOP TIP

Ensure your hair is dry when you head out for the day; in Jordan stepping out with wet hair can be viewed as an indicator of sexual availability.

📦 Pack light, loose-fitting clothing respectful of Jordan's dress code, including a headscarf for visiting mosques. A water filtration device is essential.

📅 March to May offers the most comfortable climes for exploring Jordan, with rates increasing accordingly. While desert nights can be bitter during the September to February shoulder season, there are fewer tourists to contend with – beyond Aqaba, at least.

🚌 There are three overland border crossings into Israel, but while Israeli authorities won't stamp your passport, be aware that your exit stamp from Jordan may create issues travelling on to countries such as Lebanon.

$ $

Jordan

Jordan has delighted visitors for centuries with its World Heritage Sites and inspiring desert landscapes. The nation has also been at the forefront of community-based tourism in the Middle East, with creative initiatives dotted all over the country.

From the rock-hewn city of Petra to the sprawling Roman ruins of Jerash, the dramatic moonscapes of Wadi Rum to the dazzling marine life of the Red Sea, Jordan certainly isn't short on sights. But perhaps the nation's best trait is its tradition of welcoming visitors. Whether it's bedding down with a rural family for the night or taking tea in a goat-hair tent with a nomadic Bedouin herder, there are now myriad opportunities for visitors to get a taste of Jordan's famous hospitality, with the added benefits of sidestepping the crowds and spreading your tourism dollars beyond the big hitters.

Nailing sustainable travel in Jordan

★ Check out the tourism board's 'Meaningful Travel Map' which pinpoints 12 social enterprises you may wish to support on your journey. www.myjordanjourney.com

★ Be mindful that plastic pollution is a growing issue in Jordan, with plastic bottles the key offenders.

★ Do not take your style cues from tourists wearing short skirts and strappy tops: it's respectful to keep your shoulders and knees covered at all times.

★ Skip the horse, donkey and camel rides at Petra. While

© TOM MACKIE / LONELY PLANET

local organisations say they are working with the animals' owners to improve conditions, animal welfare activists claim not enough has been done.

★ Be water wise: renewable water supply currently only meets about half of Jordan's total water consumption.

GREEN STAYS

★ Enjoy authentic Bedouin hospitality in off-grid luxury at Feynan Ecolodge in the Dana Biosphere Reserve. This solar-powered lodge acts as a base for outdoor exploration and cultural immersion: activities include mountain biking to Roman ruins and sampling cardamom-spiced coffee in a traditional goat-hair tent. www.ecohotels.me

★ In the small village of Umm Qais in Jordan's north, Beit al Baraka is a charming three-room guesthouse (complete with handcrafted beds) that engages the local community to provide activities ranging from a crash course in beekeeping to foraging for wild foods, but the organic breakfast alone is reason enough to stay. www.barakadestinations.com

GIVE BACK

★ Help empower women artisans to build meaningful careers by picking up high-quality colourful kilims and cushions from Bani Hamida Weaving Centre & Gallery in Mukawir village. To date, this women's cooperative has employed nearly 60 full-time workers from 13 villages. www.jordanriver.jo

★ Tuck into a delicious traditional meal at Beit Khairat Souf, northeast of Jerash. This social enterprise restaurant also sells delicious natural homemade food products (from exotic pickles to hand-pressed olive oil), creating additional employment opportunities for local women who have struggled to find a market for their products. www.facebook.com/baitkhayratsoof

© BRIAN SCANNELL / FEYNAN ECOLODGE

© RAED KHAWALDEH / FEYNAN ECOLODGE

Previous page, from left: Petra; salt crystals at the edge of the Dead Sea.
From far left: candlemaking workshop at Feynan Ecolodge; Nubian ibex.
Opposite: dining under the stars at Feynan Ecolodge.

INSPO AND INFO

📖 *Leap of Faith: Memoirs of an Unexpected Life* by Noor Al-Hussein (2003)
📖 Lonely Planet's *guidebook to Jordan*
🎞 *Theeb* (2014)
🎞 *17* (2017)

HANDY APP

Download the Aroundtown app for the scoop on restaurants, nightlife and events worth checking out in Amman. www.aroundtowncities.com

Ultimate sustainable travel experiences

★ Hiking at least one section of the incredible 600km (404-mile) Jordan Trail that stretches from the nation's tip to its tail, passing through Petra.

★ Looking out for neon blue agama lizards while exploring the stunning Dana Biosphere Reserve, Jordan's largest nature reserve, with a Bedouin guide.

★ Learning how locals live during a homestay experience, which can be arranged through the Al Ayoun Society, one of the first tourism cooperatives to be established in Jordan. www.facebook.com/alayounsociety.

★ Taking a wildlife safari in Shaumari Wildlife Reserve, created with the aim of reintroducing wildlife that has disappeared from the region. www.rscn.org.jo

★ Exploring the Roman ruins, museums, cafes and street life of Amman on foot.

★ Visiting Jordan's outlying Crusader castles and 'desert castles', which receive a fraction of Petra's crowds.

TOP TIP

Due to strong currents, many of Palau's dive sites are only suitable for Advanced Open Water divers. Diving gloves are allowed for gripping onto mooring lines in currents.

Practicalities

✈ Palau

🧳 Palau's tropical climate and relaxed vibe bodes well for packing light. Check ahead for potential dengue outbreaks; light, long-sleeved clothing is an excellent ecofriendly defence against mosquito bites.

📅 With calm seas between December and March attracting the bulk of tourists, consider visiting during the shoulder seasons (April to May and September to October), when the diving is still excellent and hotel rates are cheaper.

🚌 There are no overland or boat crossings.

$ $ $

Palau

The world's first country with immigration laws that promote sustainable tourism, the Micronesian nation of Palau is a true trailblazer. In order to get a visa, visitors to this 200-odd island archipelago of astounding beauty must sign a pledge to help protect it.

Like many small island nations, the economy of Palau is dependent on the ocean. Despite the impressive measures Palau's government has taken to protect it (such as turning most of its territorial waters into a marine sanctuary in 2015), rising sea levels, illegal dynamite fishing, inadequate waste disposal facilities, sand dredging, marine litter and tourism all continue to present environmental threats. With an international airport expansion due to make Palau's world-famous snorkelling and diving spots more accessible than ever in the coming years, abiding by the pledge is paramount.

Nailing sustainable travel in Pulau

★ Practise the Palau Pledge, which asks visitors to support local businesses and communities, learn about local culture and respect local customs, and not to collect marine life souvenirs, feed fish and sharks, drag fins over coral when swimming, touch or step on coral, take fruit or flowers from gardens, touch or chase wildlife, drop litter or smoke in restricted areas.

★ Pack ecofriendly sunscreen – reef-toxic sunscreens have been banned in Palau since January 2020.

★ Choose a scuba-diving operator certified by

© PUBLIC_P / SHUTTERSTOCK

international responsible diving organisation Green Fins (www.greenfins.net), and if you're planning to scuba dive at sites that require a reef hook, exercise extreme care.

★ Reduce the strain on Palau's recycling system by avoiding beverage containers – more than 11 million are imported annually. Koror's tap water is safe to drink.

GREEN STAYS

★ It might be foreign-owned, but the Palau Pacific Resort in Koror, which opened overwater villas in 2019, has some impressive ecofriendly credentials. It maintains its own source of water, generates some of its own power via solar, converts plastic waste to oil to light tiki torches, invites guests to participate in its clam propagation activities, and more. www.palaupr.com

★ On Peleliu island, the family-run Dolphin Bay Resort's seven beachside bungalows were constructed using as many natural and local materials as possible. The resort is also home to the island's first dive centre, Peleliu Divers. www.dolphinbay-resort-peleliu.com

GIVE BACK

★ Donate to the Palau Conservation Trust, which assists the government and island communities to ensure preservation of Palau's natural heritage. www.palauconservation.org

★ Australian Volunteers for International Development runs volunteer assignments in Palau that focus on a range of development areas including health, community and the environment. www.australianvolunteers.com

★ The Micronesian Conservation Trust's Micronesia Challenge, which coaches new successors to take on conservation and resource management leadership roles and responsibilities, accepts donations. www.ourmicronesia.org

© MAURITIUS IMAGES GMBH / ALAMY STOCK PHOTO

© BLUEORANGE STUDIO / SHUTTERSTOCK

Previous page, from left: Palau's uninhabited Rock Islands; world-class scuba sites abound.
From far left: Palau sunrise; snorkelling with stingless jellyfish at the Rock Islands' marine lake.
Opposite: hiking the Palau archipelago.

INSPO AND INFO

📖 *Diving and Snorkeling Guide to Palau and Yap* by Tim Rock (2018)
🎞 *Coral Compass: Fighting Climate Change in Palau* (2018)
🖥 *South Pacific* – BBC (2009)
🎤 *Pacific Beat* – ABC Radio Australia

HANDY APP

Micronesia Tour, the region's official tourism app, includes a primer on all things Palau, as well as a list of responsible travel tips. www.micronesiatour.com

Ultimate sustainable travel experiences

★ Floating amongst hundreds of non-stinging jellyfish in a landlocked marine lake, reopened in late 2018, in the uninhabited Rock Islands.

★ Scuba diving at world-class Rock Islands sites like Blue Corner and German Channel.

★ Exploring Babeldaob island slowly in a rental car: between top sights like Badrulchau Stone Monoliths and Ngardmau Waterfall, find sleepy villages and beautifully decorated bai (men's meeting houses).

★ Learning about Palau's history and culture at Koror museums including the Belau National Museum & Bai and the Etpison Museum.

★ Purchasing a bai storyboard (carved wood panel) direct from the artist – drop in on master carver Ling Inabo who runs the Tebang Woodcarving shop in Koror. www.tebangwoodcarving. com

★ Exploring the WWII relics and supporting family-run tourism establishments on the small island of Peleliu.

TOP TIP

With Vancouver, Seattle and Portland sitting on the 'West Coast Electric Highway', which has an extensive network of EV fast-charging stations, exploring the region in an EV makes sense.

Practicalities

✈ Portland; Seattle; Vancouver

🚌 Buses and trains connect Vancouver to Seattle (four hours), from where it's another 3½ hours by bus or train south to Portland.

💼 Warm layers, a raincoat and sturdy walking shoes are essentials in the Pacific Northwest. Multi-day hikers will need the tools to bury or pack out human waste.

📅 April is the time for outdoor adventures, aside from skiing. During the shoulder months of April, May and October, temperatures remain mild but crowds and prices drop off.

$ $

Pacific Northwest

Punctuated by ethereal old-growth forests, dramatic snowy peaks and a pristine coastline, the Pacific Northwest offers endless opportunities for outdoor adventure, from hiking to camping, cycling to skiing, and more.

The Pacific Northwest is also famous for its overwhelmingly green attitude to life. Renewable energy, ecofriendly transport and waste reduction strategies rule here; in 2018 Seattle became the first US city to ban plastic straws and utensils, and visitors will discover an abundance of locally produced food, wines and microbrews available across the region. Throw in buzzing arts and music scenes and a rich First Nations culture and it's easy to understand why locals don't even mind the frequent rain that helps to keep this corner of North America looking so lush and leafy.

Nailing sustainable travel in the Pacific Northwest

★ Learn and live by the Leave No Trace principles when hiking and camping in the region's spectacular green spaces.

★ Check the provenance of salmon before ordering meals; salmon farming has wreaked havoc on the marine ecosystem.

★ Follow bear and moose safety strategies to help keep wildlife (and you) safe in the Pacific Northwest wilderness.

★ Seattle might be the home of Starbucks, but your coffee money is more sustainably spent at the region's excellent local-owned coffee shops.

© DESIGN PICS / DAVID PONTON / GETTY IMAGES

★ Reduce pressure on emergency services by taking the necessary safety precautions for backcountry hiking and skiing.

GREEN STAYS

★ Roam Beyond's off-grid, portable cabin-like pods give exclusive access to the Olympic Peninsula's unparalleled wilderness without disrupting it. www.roambeyond.travel/kalaloch

★ At the ecofriendly Ace Hotel Portland, the majority of the furniture is salvaged, mattresses are made from organic materials, rooms are cleaned with non-toxic products, and minibars are stocked with local craft beer. www.acehotel.com/portland

★ On Vancouver Island, Clayoquot Wilderness Resort is ecofriendly wild luxury at its best; the tented safari camp also invites guests to get involved in wildlife habitat rehabilitation by removing marine debris from remote islands. www.wildretreat.com

GIVE BACK

★ Homelessness in Vancouver is a social crisis that has been rapidly accelerating over the last decade. One way to help is to donate money or goods to the Downtown Women's Eastside Centre – check the website to find out which items they need most. www.dewc.ca

★ Make a donation to The Whale Sanctuary Project, the first organisation focused exclusively on creating seaside sanctuaries in North America for orcas and beluga whales that are being retired from entertainment facilities or have been rescued from the ocean and need rehabilitation or permanent care. www.whalesanctuaryproject.org

© TOM CAHALAN

© MONIKA WIELAND SHIELDS / SHUTTERSTOCK

Previous page, from left: exploring the Pacific Northwest by kayak; Roosevelt elk.
From far left: Clayoquot Wilderness Resort; spyhopping orca in Puget Sound.
Opposite: Panther Creek Falls in the Columbia River Gorge.

INSPO AND INFO

📖 *The Last Wilderness* by Murray Morgan (1955)

📖 Lonely Planet's *guidebook to Washington, Oregon & the Pacific Northwest*

🎬 *Artifishal* (2019)

🎬 *V6A* (2019)

HANDY APP

The US Forest Service's Pacific Northwest Forests app provides trail maps and updates on wildfires and road conditions for all of the Pacific Northwest's national forests.
www.fs.usda.gov/r6

Ultimate sustainable travel experiences

★ **Hiking beneath towering forest canopies** in Olympic National Park and the Hoh Rain Forest, through alpine wildflower meadows in Mt Rainer National Park, and amid the exquisite Columbia River Gorge that divides Washington and Oregon.

★ **Exploring the cultural institutions, excellent restaurants and green spaces** of Portland, Seattle and Vancouver, three of the most ecofriendly cities in North America.

★ **Taking an orca-watching tour** in Washington's Puget Sound or from Vancouver Island's Telegraph Cove.

★ **Drinking your way around** the region's excellent craft breweries.

★ **Camping, skiing or hiking** in the old-growth forests surrounding Oregon's Crater Lake.

★ **Learning about First Nations culture** at the totem-pole-lined boardwalk at Albert Bay, British Columbia, and Native American history at the Makah Museum at Neah Bay on the Olympic Peninsula, which houses artifacts from one of North America's most significant archaeological finds.

TOP TIP

With Sweden home to the world's highest number of moose per capita, moose is a sustainable red meat option worth sampling (the animals are hunted free-range). Hint: it makes great meatballs.

Stockholm; Gothenburg; Malmö

🛳 Ferries connect Swedish port cities to various Nordic and Baltic Sea nations.

💼 In midsummer you'll want a reusable eye mask if you struggle to sleep in daylight hours. Shoulder seasons call for layers and wet-weather gear, while good-quality waterproof footwear is needed during the long winter months.

📅 Daytime temperatures can be surprisingly comfortable (and hotel rates lower) during the September to October shoulder season. While the winter months can be bitterly cold, the northern lights and holiday markets beckon.

🚌 Buses and trains connect Malmö to Copenhagen, Denmark, in an hour or less. Buses and trains also run to Oslo, Norway, from Gothenburg (3½ hours) and Stockholm (around 7 hours).

$ $ $

Sweden

Nowhere has embraced sustainability quite like Scandinavia. The home of the flygskam (flight shame) movement, plogging (picking up rubbish while running) and of teenage climate activist Greta Thunberg, Sweden has the region's most original eco cred.

While Sweden's summers are short, the nation's vast natural landscapes make it well worth joining locals in striking out from the big cities. The first country in the northern hemisphere to launch an ecotourism charter, Sweden's 'Nature's Best' eco-label assures the quality of hundreds of tours, meaning you can get on with exploring the nation's mossy forests, idyllic archipelagos, serene lakes and wild tundra – not to mention feasting on delicious local produce – without fretting about the impact. And with 250-plus Nordic Swan Ecolabelled hotels to choose from, finding an eco-sensitive sleep at the end of the day is a cinch, too.

Nailing sustainable travel in Sweden

★ Embrace the fresh, sustainable local seafood that forms the basis of many Swedish dishes – the country has drastically reduced its consumption of red meat in recent years.

★ Make the most of Sweden's 'freedom to roam' law, which means you can walk and camp pretty much anywhere.

★ Check the Plogga Facebook page for upcoming plogging sessions you can join around the country. www.facebook.com/plogga

© FOTO-SELECT / SHUTTERSTOCK

★ Invest in high-quality, long-lasting garments at Sweden's impressive number of ethical fashion boutiques; use the Good on You website to help locate them. www.goodonyou.eco

★ Visit Sweden as part of a longer overland trip in the Nordic region rather than flying in for a quick visit.

GREEN STAYS

★ After an experiment proved that stress levels drop significantly after a 72-hour stay in a glass-walled cabin in the Swedish countryside, the tourism board opened a collection of 72 Hour Cabins scattered across West Sweden. www.72hcabin.com

★ Rewild yourself at Kolarbyn Ecolodge, 'Sweden's most primitive hotel'. You'll cook meals over a fire, bathe in the lake and bed down in a Hobbit-style forest hut. The floating sauna makes it all worth the effort. www.wildsweden.com/kolarbyn-ecolodge

★ Housed in a retired jumbo jet conveniently parked near Stockholm's Arlanda Airport, Jumbostay is a novel low-impact, low-cost stopover accommodation option. www.jumbostay.com

GIVE BACK

★ Historically, volunteering in Sweden was difficult for non-Swedish speakers, but that's changing. IVolontärbyrån is a nationwide organisation with a programme that matches volunteers with opportunities across the country, recently extended to include English speakers. www.volontarbyran.org

★ Donate to the European Wilderness Society, whose researchers are working to find sustainable solutions to minimise human-wolf contact in Sweden. After being hunted to extinction in the 1960s, wolves began returning to the country in the early 1980s, with the current population numbering more than 300. www.wilderness-society.org

© WMARTPHOTO,MARIA WESTLING / GETTY IMAGES

© JUSTINREZNICK / GETTY IMAGES

Previous page, from left: snowbound Sámi tent; driving a team of huskies through Jukkasjärvi. **From far left:** the Northern Lights over Swedish Lapland; reindeer herd. **Opposite:** traditional Sámi storehouses .

INSPO AND INFO

📖 *Live Lagom: Balanced Living, the Swedish Way* by Anna Brones (2017)
📖 Lonely Planet's *guidebook to Sweden*
🖥 *Greta Thunberg's TED Talk* (2019)
🎞 *Life Overtakes Me* (2019)

Ultimate sustainable travel experiences

★ Signing up for a wildlife safari in central Sweden to track beavers, moose, wolves and more with Swedish wildlife tourism pioneer Wild Sweden. www.wildsweden.com

★ Foraging for berries in Sweden's forests – only an estimated 4% of wild berries are harvested each summer, so there's plenty to go round, from lingonberries to blueberries to blackcurrants, and everything in between.

★ Enjoying a traditional Sámi cultural experience in Swedish Lapland with the likes of Bjork Experience, keeping your eyes peeled for the northern lights while you're there. www.bjorkexperience.com

★ Hiking the 440km (270-mile) Kungsleden (King's Trail), Sweden's premier long-distance hiking trail, in the nation's north.

★ Exploring the stunning seascapes and traditional villages of the Gothenburg archipelago; the city is slowly rolling out electric ferries as part of its ElectriCity project.

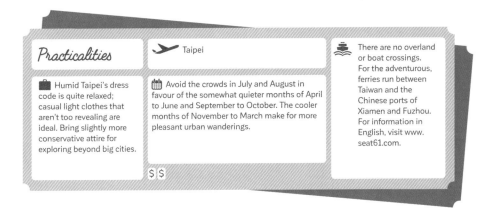

Practicalities

✈ Taipei

🧳 Humid Taipei's dress code is quite relaxed; casual light clothes that aren't too revealing are ideal. Bring slightly more conservative attire for exploring beyond big cities.

📅 Avoid the crowds in July and August in favour of the somewhat quieter months of April to June and September to October. The cooler months of November to March make for more pleasant urban wanderings.

⚓ There are no overland or boat crossings. For the adventurous, ferries run between Taiwan and the Chinese ports of Xiamen and Fuzhou. For information in English, visit www. seat61.com.

$ $

Taiwan

Formerly nicknamed 'Garbage Island' thanks to its urban waste problem, Taiwan has re-emerged as a global recycling leader. The island's war on waste has put Taiwan on the travel map and transformed it into a symbol of hope for other regions drowning in trash.

Famed for centuries as Ilha Formosa (Beautiful Isle), Taiwan packs some seriously special scenery into its 36-sq-km (14-sq-mile) land mass. From marble-walled gorges to tropical forests, mountainous hiking trails and coastal cycling routes, natural escapes are aplenty beyond Taipei. Not that it's easy to leave the squeaky clean capital with its temples, famous night markets and buzzing cafe scene, all easily accessible via the city's excellent MRT (metro) network. But what makes Taiwan really cool is its commitment to a plastic-free future, with 2020 due to see the full implementation of a ban on free plastic bags, cups, straws, utensils and disposable food containers.

Nailing sustainable travel in Taiwan

★ Respect Taiwan's wide-ranging plastic bans by refusing single-use plastics where they are still offered.

★ If you're headed to the beach, pick up some of the marine debris that plagues Taiwan's coastlines.

★ Remember to secure the appropriate permit before hiking in Taiwan's national parks (http://np.cpami.gov.tw), and avoid hiking soon after a typhoon, when landslides are common.

© LEREN LU / GETTY IMAGES

★ Exercise correct MRT etiquette: avoid blue priority seats, respect queuing protocol and lower your voice.

★ Keep all your showers short. Taiwan may receive a lot of rainfall, but the island's limited water storage means that shortages are a constant risk.

GREEN STAYS

★ As the name suggests, Star Hostel Taipei Main Station is conveniently central, but what makes this stylish hostel great is its lack of single-use plastics and passion for supporting local business, from the Eaves coffee served at breakfast to the Alchemist craft beers for sale. A healthy, low-waste breakfast is included, and there's a leafy communal lounge. www.starhostel.com.tw

★ Farm stays are becoming increasingly popular in Taiwan. A working organic farm in the southern Xinhua District, leafy Dakeng Leisure Farm also raises its own free-roaming animals and has an excellent restaurant showcasing farm-fresh ingredients. www.idakeng.com.tw

GIVE BACK

★ Animal welfare activists cheered when Taiwan banned euthanising stray pets in 2017, but the move has put extra pressure on local animal shelters. By making a donation to UK-based charity Animal Care Trust (ACT), you can help to support three sanctuaries in Taiwan started by ACT's founder. www.actforanimals.org

★ Taiwan-born social enterprise Impct Cafe invests 25% of sales in poverty-smashing businesses run by women. Grab your morning caffeine fix at its cafe in the Da'an district, and perhaps some coffee to take home – each one comes with a unique 'brick code' you can digitally 'lay' on a school project that Impct funds. www.impct.co

© IMPCT CAFE

Previous page, from left: Taipei skyline; hiking through Taiwan's lush interior forests.
From far left: the leafy communal lounge at Star Hostel Taipei; Impct Cafe barista.
Opposite: Taroko Gorge is the jewel of Taroko National Park.

© STAR HOSTEL TAIPEI

INSPO AND INFO

📖 *The Stolen Bicycle* by Wu Ming-yi (2015)
📖 Lonely Planet's *guidebook to Taiwan*
🎬 *Beyond Beauty: Taiwan from Above* (2013)
🎬 *A City of Sadness* (1989)

HANDY APP

Pleco is a nifty Chinese-English dictionary app which has both Traditional and Simplified Chinese. Just type in the English word and the results will give you both the written Taiwanese Mandarin (Pinyin) word and pronunciation.
www.pleco.com

Ultimate sustainable travel experiences

★ **Hiking or cycling** in the stunning 18km (11-mile) marble-walled Taroko Gorge, the geological jewel of the island's Taroko National Park.

★ **Learning about Taiwan's indigenous cultures,** starting with a visit to the Shung Ye Museum of Formosan Aborigines in Taipei, and then checking into a homestay run by Yami islanders on Lanyu during the flying fish season (Mar–Jun).

★ **Tackling the Mazu Pilgrimage,** a 350km (217-mile) hiking trail across Taiwan dedicated to Mazu, the maternal patron deity of the island; it starts in Dajia.

★ **Embracing the island's cycling fever** by exploring the unspoiled and sparsely populated east coast on two wheels. Try the coast road linking Hualien and Taitung, or tackle the lush green ranges of the Rift Valley.

★ **Watching Taipei light up at dusk** from the summit of Elephant Mountain, Taipei's top urban hike.

TOP TIP

Bring plenty of cash: most establishments don't take cards and the island has few ATMs, which are known to run out of cash.

Practicalities

✈ Sayak

🚢 Multiple ferries run between the Siargao port city of Dapa and Surigao City (2½ hours), the province capital.

🧳 With its casual dress code and tropical climate, you can pack light for Siargao. Surf gear can be rented locally, though consider bringing a pair of gardening gloves for beach clean-ups.

📅 Siargao's dry season (March to October) generally brings the best weather, though surfers will want to plan their visit between August and November, when the swells pick up.

$

Siargao

With its pumping surf, hidden turquoise lagoons, and an interior blanketed in coconut palms and rice paddies so green they almost glow, it's a miracle the remote Philippine island of Siargao has remined something of a travel secret for so long.

Central to this Surigao del Norte Province island's appeal is its laid-back, eco-conscious vibe. United by the Siargao Environmental Awareness (SEA) Movement, many businesses in the main tourist hub of General Luna and beyond have banned single-use plastics and have committed to minimising their impact in other ways. Refreshingly free of international chains and high-rise developments (at least for now), Siargao offers a more low-key island experience than the main tourist draws such as Boracay and El Nido; it's full of empty beaches, secret surf spots and an unusually good selection of restaurants dominated by healthy vegetarian options.

Nailing sustainable travel in Siargao

★ Practise good surf etiquette: respect locals, never drop in, know your limits, and don't reveal secret places on social media.

★ Reduce pressure on Siargao's problematic waste management system by leaving room in your suitcase to pack out as much of your own waste as you can.

★ If you're planning to explore Siargao on a motorised scooter, ensure your insurance policy covers the activity, and

© LEISA TYLER / GETTY IMAGES

always wear a helmet.

★ Spread your tourist dollars around the island by opting to stay beyond General Luna, such as in the emerging traveller hangout of Pacifico in the island's sleepy northeast.

GREEN STAYS

★ In the heart of General Luna, just steps from the beach, stylish Bravo Resort crushes glass bottles into sand, meticulously separates garbage for recycling and composts food waste. Guests receive a reusable water bottle to use during their stay, and get a 400-peso refund for every night that they use a fan rather than air-con. www.bravosiargao.com

★ German entrepreneur Carolin Dekeyser developed the idea for Nay Palad – a luxe 10-villa hideaway south of General Luna – while helping the women of Compostella, a sustainable rainforest village on Cebu, turn their ancestral skills into marketable products. Nay Palad operations also have a sustainable focus. www.naypalad.com

GIVE BACK

★ The SEA Movement hosts beach clean-ups every Saturday at 4pm (meet at Catangnan Dance Hall near Jacking Horse beach) and seeks longer-term environmental volunteers. www.seamovement.ph

★ A charity working to create sustainable island communities, hosts a beach clean-up at Pacifico on Saturdays and in Pilar on Sundays, the Sun Crew channels 100% of profits from private island tours, surf instruction and rentals to projects fighting child poverty and plastic pollution . www.thesuncrew.org

★ Challenging social issues through surfing, sports and social activities, Grom Nation also runs a not-for-profit surf school, and is always in need of surfing equipment. www.gromnationsiargao.com

© BRAVO

© BRAVO

Previous page, from left: surf's up on Siargao; recycled-plastic 'nestrest' at Nay Palad resort. **Left:** luxe Bravo resort has impeccable eco-credentials. **Opposite:** a sunset stroll back from Siargao's famous Cloud 9 surf break.

INSPO AND INFO

📖 *Barefoot in Siargao* by Christina Camingue Buo (2018)
📖 *Be Siargao* magazine
📖 Lonely Planet's **guidebook to the Philippines**
🎬 *Siargao* (2017)

HANDY APP

Read up on Siargao's surf spots and check conditions at 11 breaks around the island with the Magic Seaweed app. www.magicseaweed.com/app

Ultimate sustainable travel experiences

★ Surfing Siargao's many breaks, or learning to surf with a qualified instructor at a local surf school, such as Kermit. www.kermitsiargao. com

★ Spending a day lazing in the crystalline waters of Sugba Lagoon off the island's northwest coast, which receives less crowds than the scenic but increasingly busy Magpupungko tidal pools off the east coast.

★ Taking an island-hopping day trip with mindful operator My Siargao Guide, which includes a healthy and delicious plastic-free lunch. www.facebook.com/ mysiargaoguide

★ Starting the day with a healthy smoothie bowl at surfside Shaka Café. www. shakacafes.com

★ Getting a taste of island life beyond the tourist zone by taking a stroll in the port city of Dapa or exploring the island by motorbike.

TOP TIP

The best things in Montevideo are free, including its museums: don't miss Museo del Gaucho and the Museo Nacional de Artes Visuales.

Uruguay

After two centuries in the shadow of its neighbours, South America's smallest country is finally being recognised for its tourism potential. And with four cows to every resident, Uruguay is proving that it can be environmentally sustainable and maybe eat its beef, too.

Progressive, stable, safe and culturally sophisticated, Uruguay offers a particularly unique South American experience. While it lacks top sights, the joy of visiting reveals itself in everyday moments, from getting caught in a cow-and-gaucho traffic jam in the interior to sipping mate alongside locals at Montevideo's cafes. Despite its economy being propped up by the beef industry, Uruguay has also managed to smash its carbon footprint. More than 95% of its power is now generated by renewables, and the country continues its resolve to achieve carbon neutrality by 2030.

Nailing sustainable travel in Uruguay

★ Skip emission-intensive beef and seek out Montevideo's growing number of vegetarian restaurants instead.

★ Drink as much local wine as you like. Uruguay's wine industry is focused on sustainable winegrowing and traceability.

★ Make the most of Uruguay's vast and affordable bus system. In 2019, major bus company Copsa introduced electric buses to its fleet.

★ Ditch the smokes: Uruguay has one of the most strictly enforced smoking bans in the region, instituted by President

© OLAFSPEIER / GETTY IMAGES

Tabaré Vázquez, a practising oncologist.

★ Help Uruguay's coastline stay beautiful. Repay your hours on the sand with a mini beach clean-up.

GREEN STAYS

★ Nestled in a winery in the rolling green hills of the Maldonado region, the luxe Sacromonte is a green-roofed mountain retreat designed to have the smallest possible environmental footprint. Tour its winery in an electric buggy, set off on a hike or tuck into homegrown organic produce at the farm-to-table restaurant. www.sacromonte.com

★ With rooms taking the form of mini houseboats bobbing on a serene lagoon just north of José Ignacio, Laguna Garzón Lodge makes a fitting base for ecotourism adventures from water sports to birdwatching. There's a big focus on natural, local products at the lodge, with gourmet meals delivering a delicious taste of the region.

GIVE BACK

★ Help to monitor and protect juvenile green turtles on an eight-day volunteer placement with Karumbé, an NGO based in La Coronilla on the east coast which has been working with turtles in Uruguay for more than 20 years. www.karumbe.org

★ Manos del Uruguay is a cooperative of more than 200 independent women artisans from Uruguay's interior who create high-quality ethical and sustainable products. Support them by picking up a luxurious shawl or throw, or perhaps a cow hide-covered mate cup. Purchases can be made via the website. www.manos.uy/shop

© KSENIYA RAGOZINA / GETTY IMAGES

© KOBBY DAGAN / SHUTTERSTOCK

Previous page, from left: Colonia del Sacramento; boardwalk to the beach at Punta del Diablo.
From far left: Cabo Polonio lighthouse; Montevideo revellers during Uruguay's huge annual Carnival.
Opposite: beachfront at Punta del Este.

INSPO AND INFO

📖 *Open Veins of Latin America* by Eduardo Galeano (1971)
📖 *Tabaré* by Juan Zorrilla de San Martín (1886)
📖 Lonely Planet's *South America guidebook*
🎬 *25 Watts* (2001)

HANDY APP

Find a tasty local feed with the Food Trucks UY app, which marks the locations of Uruguay's best food trucks on a Google map as well as listing upcoming food and drink festivals. www.foodtruckuruguay.com

Ultimate sustainable travel experiences

★ Checking into one of the many ecofriendly guesthouses in the beach town of Punta del Diablo on Uruguay's untamed northern shoreline.

★ Soaking your weary travelling muscles in the hot springs near Salto.

★ Getting way off the beaten track in the remote Valle del Lunarejo protected landscape.

★ Wandering the leafy plazas and cobbled streets of picturesque Colonia del Sacramento on the Río de la Plata.

★ Losing yourself in the sand dunes and surveying the sea lions from atop the lighthouse at Cabo Polonio.

★ Touring Uruguay's newest Unesco World Heritage Site, the historic El Anglo meat-processing factory, in Fray Bentos on the Río Uruguay.

★ Wildlife-watching along the Atlantic coast, keeping an eye out for penguins, fur seals and more.

TOP TIP

Known as 'bumsters', resort-area touts can be relentless. If you're not interested in their offers, say so politely. If they're insistent, you can say you're considering reporting them to the tourist police, which has the authority to detain bumsters.

The Gambia

It may be continental Africa's smallest country, but The Gambia's natural attractions belie its size. With tourism accounting for 20% of the GDP and providing a growing source of employment, mindfully spent tourist dollars can have real impact here.

Surrounded by Senegal, The Gambia is blessed with a short but magnificent stretch of coastline, and its namesake river teems with all manner of exotic wildlife. Boat trips and overnights at riverside ecolodges reveal a wealth of wonders that include a chimpanzee island reserve. And while the country is still waiting for the progress promised by leader Adama Barrow when he ended the brutal 22-year presidency of Yahya Jammeh in 2016, the warm-hearted Gambian people more than live up to their homeland's slightly hokey moniker of 'the smiling coast of Africa'.

Nailing sustainable travel in The Gambia

★ The Gambia became an Islamic republic in 2015, and while the dress code is relaxed, it's respectful to dress modestly.

★ Don't even think about asking for a plastic bag, which are now illegal.

★ Be particularly conscious of your water and electricity use, as The Gambia experiences shortages of both.

★ Make an effort to explore beyond the beach resorts, where many visitors simply drop and flop.

★ Embrace Gambian cuisine, which is delicious and helps

© FRANS SELLIES / GETTY IMAGES

to support local farmers, who have been made increasingly vulnerable by environmental degradation, more frequent and severe droughts and rising sea levels.

★ If you sign up for a village visit, decline offers to tour schools.

GREEN STAYS

★ Founded by an expat who realised the economic benefits of tourism weren't trickling down to workers, Footsteps Eco-Lodge gives staff access to career training, paid time off, sick leave and a comfortable living wage. www.footstepsinthegambia.com

★ Listen to the hoots of the chimpanzees from one of the comfy South African-style safari tents at Chimpanzee Rehabilitation Project Camp. Prices include meals and a boat tour around the islands. www.crpthegambia.org

★ Eco-sensitive Mandina River Lodges has three luxurious lodge types, including a floating solar-powered option. www.mandinalodges.com

GIVE BACK

★ Donate to PING (People In Need Gambia), a grassroots charity that works with local people to build projects (from schools to clean water supplies) around each community's specific needs. www.pingcharity.co.uk

★ Every cent of donations made to the Gambian Schools Trust buys school resources, covers teachers' salaries and training, maintains nursery buildings, and pays for an annual shipping container to deliver supplies. www.gambianschools.org

© TREVORPLATT / GETTY IMAGES

Previous page, from left: sunset in The Gambia; Abyssinian roller. **From far left:** shades of green along the Gambia River; support The Gambia's primates with a visit to the Chimpanzee Rehabilitation Project. **Opposite:** Banjul skyline.

© DANNY159 / GETTY IMAGES

INSPO AND INFO

📖 *One Plastic Bag* by Miranda Paul (2015)
📖 *The Sun Will Soon Shine* by Sally Singhateh (2004)
📖 Lonely Planet's *guidebook to West Africa*
🎬 *Welcome to the Smiling Coast* (2016)

HANDY APP

Stay up to date with breaking local news with the Gambia News app, which also has a section dedicated to the capital Banjul.

Ultimate sustainable travel experiences

★ Visiting the Chimpanzee Rehabilitation Project, an island sanctuary on the Gambia River that's home to more than 100 chimpanzees.

★ Enjoying a low-impact seaside break at one of the Atlantic Coast's ecofriendly resorts.

★ Spotting monkeys on the nature trails that lace Bijilo Forest Park. It's worth shelling out the extra D50 for a guide, who can provide a deeper context to the plant and animal life found in this small coastal park.

★ Looking out for rare birds and giant crocodiles in the tiny Abuko Nature Reserve.

★ Sailing along mangrove-lined waterways and taking a scenic guided walk through wetlands in the Makasutu Culture Forest.

★ Recruiting a local guide to lead you on a tour of the eye-popping murals covering village homes in Kubuneh.

★ Contemplating The Gambia's slavery history at the National Museum of Albreda in the town of Juffureh.

TOP TIP

Enjoy the opportunity, rare in
Central America, to drink tap water.
It's safe to quaff almost everywhere,
though it's wise to double-check with
your accommodation host.

Practicalities

✈ San José; Liberia

🚌 It's possible to travel overland into Panama in the southeast (at Sixaola and at Paso Canoas) and into Nicaragua in the northwest (at Peñas Blancas and at Las Tablillas). You can usually cross on foot and jump on the next bus.

💼 Pack warm layers for the Monteverde Cloud Forest Reserve or San Gerardo de Dota, and consider using a natural insect repellent. Sunscreen can be expensive – consider bringing a non-toxic option from home.

📅 The rainy August to October low season brings the best swells, but if you can live without big waves aim for the quieter (and somewhat drier) shoulder seasons of May to July and November.

$ $

Costa Rica

Costa Rica is an adventure playground on an enormous scale – from spotting rare wildlife in its protected jungles to chasing waves on remote coastlines. But the country's biggest selling point is that, for the most part, tourism has been done right.

Well known for its sustainability initiatives, Costa Rica added another green feather to its cap in 2019 upon being bestowed a Champions of the Earth award, the UN's highest environmental honour, for its role in the protection of nature (conservation areas cover almost a third of the country) and its commitment to combatting climate change. With its excellent eco-sensitive tourism infrastructure, including some of the world's best eco-lodges, Costa Rica gives you a perfect taste of Central America that doesn't require working too hard to reduce your impact.

Nailing sustainable travel in Costa Rica

★ While English is widely spoken, you'll earn more respect from locals by learning a few Spanish phrases to use along the way.

★ If you've always wanted to stay in a true eco-lodge, this is your chance. Costa Rica has dozens of options at all price points.

★ Support small local business by eating at sodas. These small open-air traditional restaurants serve great-value casados (a typical dish comprising beans, rice, a small salad and a choice of meat).

★ Skip overdeveloped Pacific Coast resort areas like

© SIVELLSTRESELVA / GETTY IMAGES

Tamarindo for more low-key surf towns, including those on the southern Caribbean coast.

★ Be mindful of your water use as Costa Rica often experiences water shortages.

GREEN STAYS

★ While you could easily spend your stay lounging on the balcony of your luxe thatched-roof hut, Lapa Rios Lodge encourages guests to go on walks and wildlife cruises. www.laparios.com
★ Tucked away in the central mountains, Rancho Mastatal isn't just a great-value eco-lodge but also a sustainability education centre offering classes in everything from permaculture to natural building. www.ranchomastatal.com
★ Stay on a coffee plantation in the hills above San Jose at family-run Finca Rosa Blanca; decorated with locally handcrafted furniture, it boasts a restaurant with organic produce. www.fincarosablanca.com

GIVE BACK

★ Endangered sea turtles nest on Costa Rica's Pacific and Caribbean coasts throughout the year. Help protect them from poachers by signing up for a volunteer programme with the likes of Osa Conservation (osaconservation.org) or perhaps 'adopt' a turtle via the Sea Turtle Conservancy. www.conserveturtles.org
★ In the hills north of San Jose, the not-for-profit Toucan Rescue Ranch is dedicated to rescuing, rehabilitating, and releasing wildlife. It runs a four-week volunteering programme, or you can 'adopt' a member of your favourite species for US$100. www.toucanrescueranch.org

Previous page, from left: Playa Negra on Costa Rica's coast; three-toed sloth.

Clockwise from left: classes at Rancho Mastatal; kinkajou and keel-billed toucan at the Toucan Rescue Ranch. **Opposite:** rainforest view from Rancho Mastatal.

INSPO AND INFO

📖 *Costa Rica: A Traveler's Literary Companion* edited by Barbara Ras (1994)
📖 Lonely Planet's *guidebook to Costa Rica*
🎬 *A Bold Peace* (2016)
🎬 *The Goose with the Golden Eggs: Tourism on Costa Rica's Pacific Coast* (2014)

© RANCHO MASTATAL

Ultimate sustainable travel experiences

★ **Looking out for wildlife while hiking** the jungly trails that lace Parque Nacional Volcán Arenal and the wilder trails of remote Parque Nacional Corcovado.

★ **Touring organic, family-run coffee plantations** in the central highlands.

★ **Canoeing the canals of Parque Nacional Tortuguero,** where you can get up close with caimans, river turtles, sloths and more without disturbing them.

★ **Studying the art of permaculture and holistic living** while staying on one of Costa Rica's organic farms that double as sustainability learning centres.

★ **Discovering why Costa Rica is famous for its white-water rafting** by hitting the rapids on the Pacuare, Reventazón, Sarapiquí or Tenorio Rivers.

★ **Perfecting your downward dog** in Nosara, the nation's yoga capital, where sustainability is championed by the local-government-supported Sustainable Nosara group.

TOP TIP

Renting a car, or travelling around by local bus, is the best way to explore the island's sustainable tourism offerings. Along the way, discover public beaches and traditional villages beyond the resorts.

Practicalities

✈ Sir Seewoosagur Ramgoolam Airport

🛳 There are no overland or boat crossings.

🧳 The island's tropical climate calls for light, comfortable clothing year-round; bring a long skirt, trousers or a sarong to wear into Hindu temples.

📅 Avoid the island's humid December to February high season and plan to arrive in the October to November shoulder season, when diving visibility is excellent.

$ $

Mauritius

As early Dutch sailors wiped out much of its wildlife, and French colonisers replaced forests with sugarcane plantations, Mauritius isn't an obvious eco-hotspot. But some remarkable low-impact experiences await those prepared to seek them out.

The Indian Ocean island nation might have been a little late to the sustainable tourism game, but the tide is turning. In 2019, the Mauritian Standard on Sustainable Tourism was recognised by the Global Sustainable Tourism Council, offering travellers an easy way to check if tourism products meet the local benchmark.

Venture beyond the many resort areas and you'll discover a growing number of opportunities to be immersed in nature and the island's rich culture. Making these experiences more accessible is Mauritius Conscious. Launched in 2017, Mauritius' first travel agency dedicated to sustainable travel crafts itineraries that pair the island's best outdoor adventures and cultural experiences – from kayaking through mangrove forests to urban street-food tours – with low-impact eco-lodge and guesthouse stays.

© OHRIMALEX / GETTY IMAGES

Nailing sustainable travel in Mauritius

★ Take the local bus if you're planning to visit traffic-choked Port Louis, one of the island's most underrated culinary destinations.

★ Pack out recyclables to dispose of thoughtfully at home – only 6.25% of Mauritius' rubbish is currently recycled.

★ Stay hydrated with tap water, which is safe to drink.

★ Bed down in local-run guesthouses instead of foreign-owned beach resorts.

★ Skip captive wildlife attractions and Tamarin Bay's poorly regulated dolphin-watching tours in favour of spotting wildlife in natural parks and conservation areas.

GREEN STAYS

★ The island's only glamping operation, Otentic has two stunning ecofriendly properties: Otentic River in Grand River and the more rustic Otentic Mountain in the Bambous Virieux valley. Both were constructed with ultra-sustainable materials, and the communal meals made with homegrown organic produce are some of the best you'll taste on Mauritius. www.otentic.mu

★ Set in a tiny 'village' of local businesses that celebrate products and produce sourced on the island (including a restaurant, boutique and eco-tour operator), charming Vanilla House makes an excellent base in the Black River district. www.mauritius-guest-house.com

GIVE BACK

★ Even if you don't visit Île aux Aigrettes, consider a contribution to the Mauritian Wildlife Foundation, which will help fund its wildlife conservation and restoration initiatives. www.mauritian-wildlife.org

★ Help empower 450 vulnerable Mauritian children and their families to become active citizens by donating via GlobalGiving to an initiative run by local NGO, Terrain for Interactive Pedagogy through Arts. www.globalgiving.com

★ Buy a T-shirt or donate online to support the work of non-profit Reef Conservation Mauritius, which focuses its efforts on conserving and restoring the island's coastal and marine environment. www.reefconservation.mu

© OTENTIC RIVER

© JACQUES DE SPÉVILLE

Previous page, from left: Mauritius' Unesco-listed Le Morne Brabant; kitesurfing at Le Morne.
From far left: sustainable living at Otentic; echo parakeet at the Mauritian Wildlife Foundation.
Opposite: jungle huts at Otentic Mountain.

INSPO AND INFO

📖 *Dodo: From Extinction to Icon* by Errol Fuller (2002)
📖 *Island Kitchen* by Selina Periampillai (2019)
📖 Lonely Planet's *guidebook to Mauritius, Réunion & Seychelles*
🎬 *Lonbraz Kann* (2014)

Ultimate sustainable travel experiences

★ **Being a conservationist for a day** on Île aux Aigrettes with the Mauritian Wildlife Foundation, an NGO working to save several endemic wildlife and plant species, including the critically endangered Mauritius olive white-eye. www.mauritian-wildlife.org

★ **Learning more about Mauritian history and culture** on a food, village or craft-making tour with My Moris. www.mymoris.mu

★ **Hiking the many trails** that criss-cross Black River Gorges National Park in the island's rugged southwest.

★ **Riding an e-bike** up to the mountain hamlet of Chamarel with its spectacular waterfall and Terres de 7 Couleurs.

★ **Renting a kayak to explore the island's lagoons** on your own, or signing up for a guided paddle in the remote north with Yemaya Adventures. www.yemayaadventures.com

★ **Skipping motorised aquatic adventures** and learning how to kitesurf in Le Morne.

TOP TIP

Be sure to greet people when entering a shop or business, and engage in a little chit-chat before making a request of a local. Failing to do so is considered rude.

Practicalities

✈️ Douglas–Charles; Canefield

🚢 Ferries connect Dominica with Guadeloupe (2¼ hours), Martinique (2¼ hours), and St Lucia (4¼ hours).

💼 Invest in a good-quality dry bag or waterproof phone case to keep your devices dry on boat trips and hikes rather than using plastic bags. A water filtration device will also come in handy in Dominica, which struggles with water sanitation.

📅 The island's driest months (February to June) are its most popular, but the November to January shoulder season is also an excellent time to visit. Aim for the week leading up to Independence Day (3 November) to witness the vibrant celebration of local heritage.

$ $ $

Dominica

Locals joke that if Columbus returned to the Caribbean, the 'Nature Isle' is the only island he'd recognise. Dominica's lures eco-adventurers with a boiling lake, rainforest-shrouded volcanoes, hot springs, superb diving and the region's first long-distance hiking trail.

An English-speaking former British colony wedged between francophone Guadeloupe and Martinique, Dominica is also on a different path to its neighbours in development terms, with no big cruise terminal nor an airport that can take even medium-haul flights – at least not yet. This means the island's natural and cultural heritage – Dominica is home to the Caribbean's only remaining population of pre-Columbian Caribs – has been far better preserved than elsewhere in the Lesser Antilles. Still recovering from the devastation wreaked by Hurricane Maria in 2017, which damaged 90% of the island's infrastructure, Dominica also needs tourism dollars more than most Caribbean destinations.

Nailing sustainable travel in Dominica

★ Stay in local-owned accommodation rather than one of the big international hotels that are beginning to open on the island.

★ Extend your trip to explore your transit stop en route to Dominica. Flights typically arrive via hubs including Antigua, Barbados, Guadeloupe, Martinique, Puerto Rico, St-Martin/Sint Maarten and St Lucia.

© SECRET BAY

★ Driving is the most convenient way to explore the island, but consider using local buses, which can be flagged down anywhere.

★ Make a concerted effort to eat local produce to help support hard-working farmers.

★ Encourage Dominica's efforts to eradicate single-use plastics; plastic bags were banned

GREEN STAYS

★ Perched on a cliff above the sea near Portsmouth, and developed without heavy machinery Secret Bay is an intimate eco-luxury retreat with six villas, a wellness pavilion and a fine-dining restaurant showcasing indigenous herbs grown on-site, and you can even have a shot at spearing an invasive lionfish for your supper. www.secretbay.dm

★ Manicou River's cluster of beautifully furnished, hand-built wooden cottages near Portsmouth have ocean views and are 100% energy and water self-sufficient. www.manicouriver.com

★ Tucked in the jungle near Roseau, Cocoa Cottage has rooms decorated with local artwork and serves delicious organic meals. www.cocoacottages.com

GIVE BACK

★ Donate to the Dominica Hurricane Maria Relief Fund, an appeal launched by the Dominica High Commission to raise funds for everything from building materials to medical supplies. www.dominicarelief.org

★ UK-based charity DominicaFirst, which works to limit the hardship caused by natural disasters, also takes donations. You can also volunteer for the organisation in the UK (check the website for skills required) or get involved by attending fundraising events. www.dominicafirst.com

From left: the cathedral of Our Lady of Fair Haven in Roseau, Dominica's capital; spot humpback whales scuba diving.
Opposite: rooms amid the rainforest at Cocoa Cottage.

INSPO AND INFO

🎦 *Uncivilized* (2019)
📖 *The Dominica Story* by Lennox Honychurch (1995)
📖 *The Orchid House* by Phyllis Shand Allfrey (1953)
📖 Lonely Planet's *Caribbean Islands guidebook*

© SECRET BAY

Ultimate sustainable travel experiences

★ Ticking off the great hikes of Dominica – from the 14-section Waitukubuli National Trail, the Caribbean's only long-distance route, to the famous Boiling Lake day hike – with the free Official Trail Hiker's Log Book and Passport.

★ Connecting with the ancient traditions of indigenous Kalinago people at the east coast Kalinago Barana Autê heritage village. www.kalinagoterritory.com/attractions/the-kalinago-barana-aute

★ Chasing waterfalls, particularly Middleham Falls, Dominica's highest waterfall, the easily accessible twin Trafalgar Falls where you can take a dip in the pools below, and the waterfall at the end of stunning swim to.

★ Finding out why Dominica is one of the Caribbean's top scuba-diving destinations.

★ Lazing about drinking rum punch – sans plastic straw – on palm-fringed Batibou Beach.

★ Relaxing in the hot sulphur springs amid stunning scenery in the verdant village of Wotten Waven.

AFTER YOUR TRIP

Making your impact count

WRITE BACK

Did you promise a local guide or community member that you'd write to them or perhaps send them some photos or supplies when you returned home? Keep your word by following through.

Sustainable travel doesn't end when you get home. Small post-trip actions can encourage others to join the movement, and lay foundations for your future adventures.

TALK ABOUT IT

You won't need much persuasion, but when regaling friends and family with stories from your trip, be sure to highlight the more sustainable travel experiences you enjoyed and explain what made these experiences so special. By starting conversations about sustainable travel, particularly with people who may not know much about it, travellers can influence others to make more sustainable travel decisions.

POST ABOUT IT

With most people trusting online reviews as much as friends, the travel content you post on your social media channels can have considerable impact. Keep that in mind when deciding which travel memories you're going to share, and how you plan to share them.

GIVE MEANINGFUL GIFTS

Chances are your mates have enough novelty fridge magnets. By presenting loved ones with sustainable gifts bought on your travels and sharing the stories behind them, you can help to place more value on sustainable local handicrafts and other products.

© SUN_SHINE / SHUTTERSTOCK

WRITE A REVIEW

Did you have an incredible sustainable tourism experience you'd love other travellers to know about? By writing a review on an online forum you can help to encourage other travellers to support that particular provider or operator. Similarly, if you think there is room for a tourism business you experienced to improve, you may wish to leave a constructive review to help warn others and perhaps prompt the company to raise its game.

HONE YOUR SUSTAINABLE LIVING SKILLS

Incorporating more sustainable practices into your day-to-day life – from eliminating single-use plastics from your home to taking public transport more often – not only smooths the way to making more sustainable choices on the road but can also help to mitigate the emissions of future trips.

STORE YOUR GEAR WISELY

If good-quality travel gear is looked after, it should last for years. When returning home from a trip, ensure your kit is properly cleaned and mended if needed, then carefully stored. Remove batteries from travel gadgets so they don't corrode the devices while not in regular use, and remember to air out travel clothes and shoes, and rinse snorkelling gear occasionally, to make sure the items will hold their form for many adventures to come.

THE POWER OF FEEDBACK

Perhaps a hotel you stayed in was not as ecofriendly as it marketed itself to be. Or maybe you travelled with an operator who included an excursion on your itinerary that wasn't particularly sustainable. By sharing your concerns directly with the manager, perhaps via email when you get home, you can help to inspire change. Without pressure from travellers, tourism businesses that aren't operating as responsibly as they could be have little incentive to improve their operations.

For more serious issues, such as a suspicion that a so-called sanctuary you visited might be involved in wildlife trafficking, or concerns that an operator was taking advantage of its staff, you may wish to refer the issue to an animal welfare charity or make a complaint to the relevant government authority, such as the tourism board.

INDEX

Published in November 2020 by Lonely Planet Global Limited
CRN 554153
www.lonelyplanet.com
ISBN 978 1 78868 947 2
© Lonely Planet 2020
Printed in China
10 9 8 7 6 5 4 3 2 1

Publishing Director Piers Pickard
Associate Publisher Robin Barton
Editors Dora Ball, Christina Webb, Monica Woods, Polly Thomas
Art Director Daniel Di Paolo
Layout and Picture Research Jo Dovey
Proofreading Molly Ahuja
Print Production Nigel Longuet
Cover illustration © Muti / Folio Art

Written by Sarah Reid, who is an award-winning travel writer and editor with a passion for sustainable adventure travel. She writes for leading travel publishers around the world (see sarahreid.com.au for her latest articles and books) and runs sustainable travel website ecotravelist.com. Follow her low-impact adventures on Instagram @ecotravelist.

STAY IN TOUCH lonelyplanet.com/contact

AUSTRALIA The Malt Store, Level 3, 551 Swanston St, Carlton, Victoria 3053. T: 03 8379 8000

IRELAND Digital Depot, Roe Lane (off Thomas St), Digital Hub, Dublin 8, D08 TCV4

USA Suite 208, 155 Filbert Street, Oakland, CA94607. T: 510 250 6400

UNITED KINGDOM 240 Blackfriars Rd, London SE1 8NW. T: 020 3771 5100

Although the authors and Lonely Planet have taken all reasonable care in preparing this book, we make no warranty about the accuracy or completeness of its content and, to the maximum extent permitted, disclaim all liability from its use.

Paper in this book is certified against the Forest Stewardship Council™ standards. FSC™ promotes environmentally responsible, socially beneficial and economically viable management of the world's forests.